D0970950

business
and **government**
in canada

GOVERNANCE SERIES

Governance is the process of effective coordination whereby an organization or a system guides itself when resources, power, and information are widely distributed. Studying governance means probing the pattern of rights and obligations that underpins organizations and social systems; understanding how they coordinate their parallel activities and maintain their coherence; exploring the sources of dysfunction; and suggesting ways to redesign organizations whose governance is in need of repair.

The Series welcomes a range of contributions — from conceptual and theoretical reflections, ethnographic and case studies, and proceedings of conferences and symposia, to works of a very practical nature — that deal with problems or issues on the governance front. The Series publishes works both in French and in English.

The Governance Series is part of the publications division of the Program on Governance and Public Management at the School of Political Studies. Nine volumes have previously been published within this series. The Program on Governance and Public Management also publishes electronic journals: the quarterly www.optimumonline.ca and the biannual www.revuegouvernance.ca

Editorial Committee

business
and government
in canada

Jeffrey Roy

The University of Ottawa Press

Ottawa

NATIONAL LIBRARY OF CANADA CATALOGUING IN PUBLICATION

Roy, Jeffrey

Business and government in Canada / Jeffrey Roy.

(Governance series)
Includes bibliographical references and index.
ISBN 978-0-7766-0658-3

1. Industrial policy--Canada. 2. Business and politics--Canada.
I. Title. II. Series: Governance series (Ottawa, Ont.)

HD3616.C32R69 2007   322'.30971   C2007-903948-0

Published by the University of Ottawa Press, 2007
542 King Edward Avenue
Ottawa, Ontario K1N 6N5
www.uopress.uottawa.ca

The University of Ottawa Press acknowledges with gratitude the support extended to its publishing list by Heritage Canada through its Book Publishing Industry Development Program, by the Canada Council for the Arts, by the Canadian Federation for the Humanities and Social Sciences through its Aid to Scholarly Publications Program, by the Social Sciences and Humanities Research Council, and by the University of Ottawa. We also gratefully acknowledge the Center on Governance at the University of Ottawa whose financial support has contributed to the publication of this book.

CONTENTS

PREFACE

The purpose of this short book is to engage students in a dialogue on the importance of interactions and interrelations between government and business. Although most countries in the world now embrace "good governance" as a central tenet of development and prosperity, many tensions and choices remain. Even as most countries readily accept the importance of collaboration between the public and private sectors, many risks and diverging interests remain. In short, while the ideology of governance is less polarized than in recent decades, the conduct and design of sectoral relations are both more strategic and more nuanced and, arguably, more interesting as a result.

It is this challenge of conducting and designing governance in ways that transcend or enjoin business and government that is the central focus of this book. Three divergent yet complementary perspectives on the relational nexus between these sectors serve as a platform. The perspectives have been developed by three leading Canadian scholars in their fields, all of whom have contributed to my own learning on the topics at hand. My biases are no doubt exposed as the book progresses, due in no small measure to my good fortune in having apprenticed directly with one member of this eminent group.

Indeed, this book stems from the importance and enjoyment of teaching government-business relations in management programs oriented to either business or government managers or aspirants—or, in the best of all worlds, a mixing of these groups. All too often academic specialization creates a false dichotomy between the public and private realms, resulting in missed opportunities for students and diminished capacities for collaborative innovation and learning for the country as a whole.

Fortunately, over the past decade, I have been blessed with the opportunity to try to bridge this cognitive gap with both undergraduate and graduate students alike. It is my hope that our classroom discussions, from which I have benefited tremendously, have also served them well by providing some of the tools necessary for sound navigation in today's environment of complexity and change; it is to them that I dedicate this book with gratitude for so many rewarding moments of shared learning. A note of thanks must also be extended to colleagues and reviewers of early drafts of this text as well as to the highly competent editing and production team at the University of Ottawa Press. Despite their best efforts, all errors and omissions are solely my responsibility.

INTRODUCTION

This book examines five of the most critical thematic challenges confronting business and government in Canada, both separately and collectively, in today's increasingly networked governance environment. The five challenges, explained more fully below, are corporate governance, lobbying and influence, security and privacy, public-private partnerships, and geography and development. Underpinning all of these challenges is the following premise: *the boundaries between business and government are increasingly fluid and often transcended. Yet it remains important to both acknowledge and make the appropriate usage of the fundamental differences between each sector, which dictate the need for boundaries in the first place.*

Established and maintained for different purposes, each sector features a unique set of structures and cultures that reflects its broad purpose and contribution to the stability and collective fortunes of a particular jurisdiction, most often but not exclusively a country. For government, this uniqueness stems from the pursuit of objectives and outcomes deemed to be in the "public interest." Typically, the public interest is defined as a collective agenda, involving various forms of actions or services that impact all members of a jurisdiction. Accountable to the citizenry as a whole, the public sector is a political arena in which competing interests clash and are then reconciled through mechanisms overseen by elected officials—acting as representatives of the people.

Business, by contrast, is driven by a "private interest" of the owners of capital who have invested resources in an enterprise seeking to create and exploit opportunities in a competitive marketplace. Generating an economic return (a surplus or profit) is not only the primary objective but also the basis of sustaining what is ultimately a choice by owners to commit to operating their enterprise. Unlike the typically broad scope of government, businesses or companies can serve a very narrow customer base, although today the expansion of markets both within and beyond national borders affords greater opportunities for growth and diversification as well.

These characterizations do not always hold true, however, since each sector may at times confront countervailing pressures. For businesses, stakeholder capitalism in its various guises, such as corporate social responsibility and the balanced scorecard, seeks to widen the prism of private sector accountability to issues and interests that might typically be viewed as the domain of government. The public sector, similarly, faces constant pressure to manage itself more efficiently and effectively, with the private sector often serving as a comparative model. Some governments even explicitly aim to become more businesslike, while others are more subtle in importing managerial practices and governance models from the private realm.

Such pressures for comparison and, at times, convergence stem from the increasingly demanding environments within which business and government operate. Be they from citizens and special interest groups in the political realm or consumers and investors in the marketplace, both private and public sector organizations face heightened demands for accountability. These demands often stem from governance failures that are both wider in impact and amplified in coverage by intensifying and often instantaneous media coverage.

Private sector scandals such as Enron, WorldComm, and Nortel drive debates about the corporate governance regimes of companies, much as government mishaps such as the sponsorship scandal fuel questions and debates about democratic governance. The operative word here across both is *governance,* suggesting that while each retains its distinctive purposes and features, there are also commonalities in creating mechanisms for accountability and control on the one hand and performance on the other.

Governance may be defined as the means of coordination in a world where power and information are increasingly distributed (Paquet 1997, 2005). The latter part of this definition, a networked world, underlines the complexity of both decision making and accountability within and outside organizations, in an environment that some have termed the "age of transparency" (Tapscott and Ticoll 2003). The explosion of a new digital infrastructure and the Internet in particular comprise a key distributive force in this regard.

This generic definition of governance means that while it is useful as an umbrella term, it is also necessary to be more precise in its application in reference to the conduct of (1) a unique organization, private or public; (2) a specific sector (democracy and the realm of government or competitive markets, such as the business realm); or (3) a jurisdictional system, such as a city, a country, or even the world as a whole (i.e., global governance).

Within the confines of a country such as Canada, the primary focus of this book is an exploration of the systemic dynamics of intersectoral governance that shape the collective performance of a holistic jurisdiction nationally. The first chapter begins this exploration with a consideration of governance within the respective sectoral realms of government and business (with some cross-fertilization resulting). The remainder of the book then dissects Canadian governance into specific thematic challenges that are intertwined with both direct and indirect forms of intersectoral interaction.

In other words, our interest lies not in dissecting the specific governance dynamics within each sector but in understanding those processes enjoining them. How they are *independent* is one aspect of this storyline, but so is how they *influence* one another, while another aspect is comprised of approaches and mechanisms that recognize *interdependence* across increasingly fluid sectoral boundaries when shared pursuits rival or ultimately trump separate interests.

INDEPENDENCE, INFLUENCE, AND INTERDEPENDENCE

To fulfill this mission, it is first necessary to provide some conceptual underpinnings of business-government relations: fortunately, there are some useful foundations from the Canadian scene to do so. I adopt three separate perspectives and presentations of the relational dynamics between business and government to frame this introductory discussion and the subsequent storylines of the chapters. Each perspective has been developed in recent years by a leading Canadian scholar, and as we shall see each one provides valuable guidance for examining specific issues and agendas of each sector and how they interact and determine the fate of a particular jurisdiction.

Independence
The first conceptual perspective comes from the late Jane Jacobs, an American-born citizen of Canada perhaps best known for her writings on the workings of cities and urban life. However, her 1992 book entitled *Systems of Survival* makes an important contribution to the understanding of business and government as separate and distinct domains or "syndromes," to use Jacobs' chosen term.[1]

The book is written as a dialogue among a group of diverse individuals who came together to explore the moral underpinnings of modern societies. A central tenet of the book is the presentation of the private and public spheres as two independent worlds, depicted and contrasted as the guardian and the commercial syndromes. In each case, a set of principles and values defines the purpose and behaviour of actors, be they individuals or organizations, operating within institutionalized boundaries. The result is a form of covenant governing the actions of each group that, in turn, translate into market-driven versus government-based incentives and choices.

The following traits summarize Jacobs' two syndromes:

A. COMMERCIAL MORAL SYNDROME	B. GUARDIAN MORAL SYNDROME
• Shun force	• Shun trading
• Come to voluntary agreements	• Exert prowess
• Be honest	• Be obedient and disciplined
• Collaborate easily with strangers and aliens	• Adhere to tradition
• Compete	• Respect hierarchy
• Respect contracts	• Be loyal
• Use initiative and enterprise	• Take vengeance
• Be open to inventiveness and novelty	• Deceive for the sake of the task
• Be efficient	• Make rich use of leisure
• Promote comfort and convenience	• Be ostentatious
• Dissent for the sake of the task	• Disperse largesse
• Invest for Productive Purposes	• Be exclusive
• Be industrious	• Show fortitude
• Be thrifty	• Be fatalistic
• Be optimistic	• Treasure honor

Two important assertions arise from this depiction and its discourse-based application to modern governance systems. First, individuals are naturally drawn and more suitable to one sphere of activity or the other; second, mixing individuals and organizational activities from both spheres is inherently dangerous, leading to what Jacobs terms "monstrous moral hybrids" (80). As a result, a key message derived from this narrative is the importance of separateness between business and government, in large part due to the dangers of inappropriate mixing or collusion.

Taken at face value, Jacobs' presentation merely serves to reinforce the important contrast between public purpose and private gain. It bears noting, however, that this seemingly obvious message came after a decade of largely conservative rule in most Anglo-Saxon countries during which the rise of new public management strongly encouraged the importation of business practices and values (and in many cases people) into government. Moreover, within the private sector, the growing movement toward sustainable development was based on embracing the guardian-like responsibilities of business organizations to exercise greater ecological sensitivity.

It seemed legitimate to Jacobs to question whether combining the two syndromes would be a workable proposition. A contemporary example, former Italian prime minister Silvio Berlusconi, seems to support her caution. Elected to political office as one of the country's leading commercial owners of broadcast media, his unusually pronounced mixing of private interests with public office resulted in *The Economist* describing him as "unfit" to lead the country (and going so far as to allege links to organized crime).

Yet defenders of Berlusconi downplayed such tensions as slander or cultural bias, in many cases pointing to the utility of a proven leader from the private sector willing to tackle a hostile and even dysfunctional political system badly in need of reform (also pointing to the absence of a firm judicial conviction). His five years of tumultuous rule (ending in the spring of 2006) come about as close as one can get to a perilous example of Jacobs' monstrous hybrid from one of the world's leading industrialized countries. Yet the Italian example is hardly unique, since no G-8 country is free of scandals or accusations of inappropriate conduct rooted in mixes of public and private purposes.

The risks are even greater in developing nations and countries in transition. Jacobs' portrayal of the dangers of hybrid activity would find much resonance in jurisdictions across Eastern Europe and the former Soviet Union, where the absence of strong boundaries between commercial and guardian enterprises has been fertile ground for corruption and mismanagement. The problem faced by many such jurisdictions is that the lack of historical balance between separate state and market spheres of activity has meant that the abandonment of communism in favour of capitalism has occurred in an ideological and institutional vacuum.

Similar challenges and circumstances exist in many regions of the world. Indeed, they fuel efforts by global bodies, such as the OECD and its ideological affiliates, to promote more transparent and agreed-upon boundaries between markets and state, commercial enterprise and government-run entities, and individual interests that might otherwise become unfairly fused, resulting in the very sorts of hybrid organizations about which Jacobs provided warnings.

No country can be entirely immune to perilous fusions of public office and private gain. Jacobs was not naive enough to believe that individuals should always be forced to choose between the two contrasting spheres of activity. Her objective was instead to underline the need to ensure sophistication and vigilance in reminding ourselves and our societies of the appropriateness of boundaries between sectors that exist for fundamentally different purposes.

Just as the mixing of public and private interests has arguably become more common — perhaps unavoidably so in light of today's governance complexities — so too there is a need to

(1) ensure that safeguards are in place to govern individual and organizational conduct both within and across each sphere;

(2) design and implement appropriate mechanisms for evaluation and judgment that account for the separate — and at times interrelated — pursuits of public and private interests; and

(3) foster awareness of and dialogue on where the appropriate boundaries lie between commercial and guardian endeavours in light of changing socioeconomic, political, and technological circumstances.

Accordingly, Jacobs argues, indirectly through the pronouncements of a fictional character, for a moral awareness that enables humans to make effective use of both syndromes. The ideal governance environment, then, allows individuals to both pursue and combine various forms of commercial and guardian activities in a manner that is both ethical and productive to society as a whole. In other words, transcending boundaries requires careful contemplation of why such boundaries exist in the first place as well as the potential pitfalls of integrative governance models.

Influence

As a consequence, many capitalist jurisdictions in the OECD world — particularly Anglo-Saxon countries — have responded to Jacobs' analysis by seeking greater clarity and separation between the private and public realms. This favouring of sectoral independence, while not without strengths in seeking to limit corruption and inappropriate hybrids, comes at a cost, however: specifically, a poor level of communication and mutual understanding between industry and government. This gap between the sectors thus becomes an arena of influence where intermediaries are deployed to further interests and shape decisions on either side.

Here is where Jacobs' foundation of commercial and guardian syndromes underpins the second of our three perspectives, William Stanbury's (1993) typology of business-government relations. Stanbury's acceptance of sectoral distinctions serves as a conceptual basis for depicting how these two fundamentally different sets of actors interact with one another — as they invariably must when guardian responsibilities and commercial interests overlap or collide.

A chief actor in Stanbury's policy arena is therefore the lobbyist — the professional intermediary hired by business interests (within his template, though, lobbying need not be on behalf of private enterprise) to exert influence within the realm of government. It is no accident that contemporary usage of the term "lobbyist" is derived from and remains most firmly entrenched in those Anglo-Saxon jurisdictions, such as Great Britain and the United States, most overtly seeking separation between industry and government. As governance has become more complex (not unlike the moral quandaries presented by Jacobs), the need and opportunities for lobbyists grow.

Yet there are also two contrasting sets of reasons that would explain a more limited presence of formalized, professional lobbying in a given jurisdiction: transparency and secrecy. With respect to transparency, in countries such as those of Scandinavia, where the policy arena is comparatively more open and transparent (due to the laws and political customs of these countries[2]), individuals and organizations become empowered with awareness and influence (either directly via political processes or indirectly via stakeholder groups) that diminish the needs and possibilities for professional intermediaries.

The alternative explanation, secrecy, finds resonance in those countries and cultures where close ties between industry and government are normalized but hidden from the public purview. In France, for example, lobbying has been rejected until recently as a legitimate activity, since collaboration between the public and private sectors occurs more directly—and often covertly—through shared networks and fused organizational models. This sort of public-private model worked extremely well in the latter half of the twentieth century as France built a leading economic and technological infrastructure: it was subsequently carried to the European level, where this concerted mentality would underpin the success of Airbus as a rival to Boeing.

Today—and here France is most certainly not alone—the absence of transparency implied by such collusion finds itself increasingly at odds with the pressures stemming from wider media scrutiny and more direct forms of public accountability. In terms of Stanbury's policy arena, while one has long existed in France, it has been reserved for select players and elite organizations operating in networks that have been shielded from public oversight. Whether the resulting hybrid models merit being termed "monstrous" (i.e., Jacobs' vocabulary) is clearly a politically contested notion, one that must also be situated within a specific historical context. But many French observers would likely agree with a Jacobs-inspired notion that a bit more clarity, more independence, and more separate and direct accountability within both industry and government are warranted.

Despite the potential for wider transparency to diminish the role of lobbyists, countries such as the United States and Canada find themselves with a policy arena that is sufficiently inclusive of separate market and government processes on the one hand and limited degrees of transparency on the other, a combination that serves lobbyists quite well. The result is that while lobbying may be interpreted as indicative of a healthy and desirable level of freedom of expression and organization across the private and public spheres, it is also not without its own drawbacks in terms of both perception and performance. Chief among them pertain to the ethical conduct of lobbyists and resulting structural concerns about public policy making skewed to unevenly or unfairly (or both) represented interests.

Accordingly, lobbying is a key dimension of business-government relations today, one with both organizational-specific dimensions (i.e., how do firms and industries attempt to shape government decisions in some manner?) and systemic dimensions (i.e., how well is the governance system for a given jurisdiction performing overall in terms of fair access and ethical decision making?). Such themes are explored more fully in chapter 2.

Interdependence

An alternative depiction of business-government relations that is equally concerned with systemic performance is less concerned with specific information flows and strategies of influence than with overall learning and mutual adjustment. This "co-evolutionary" perspective of private, public, and civic spheres (the last also referred to as civil society, the non-profit or third sector[3]) respects the need for sectoral boundaries while also emphasizing the manner in which sectors are interdependent—not only influencing one another according to their own specific agendas and structures but also engaging in concerted processes, the resilience of which determines the collective governance performance of a jurisdiction as a whole.

Central to co-evolutionary performance is therefore social or collective learning, a process of mutual adjustment that comes about as three distinct sectors—private, public, and civic—act not only individually according to their own specific ethos (competition in the marketplace, coercion in the state, and reciprocity in civil society) but also collectively. To illustrate, Gilles Paquet (1996-97, 1997, 1999; Archibald, Galipeau, and Paquet 1990) adopted a modified governance triangle derived from the theoretical underpinnings of institutional economist Kenneth Boulding. The Boulding triangle is construed as follows:

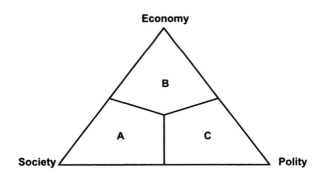

Importantly, the precise boundaries separating the sectors—and thus point "K" as the intersection of these boundaries—are in constant flux from impacts both large and small in a given jurisdictional environment. For instance, a natural disaster of one sort or another can dramatically, albeit hopefully temporarily, cause the market sector (economy) to contract in favour of government action (polity) and/or the self-organizing capabilities of citizens and communities (society). Often more subtly, democratic elections, economic growth, and policy shifts driven by either foreign or domestic circumstances can alter the relative sectoral balance.

Paquet's depiction of these interdependencies is particularly apt in portraying the systemic governance challenges of a jurisdiction as a set of many different types of organizations and institutions. Indeed, while today the term "governance" is nearly ubiquitous in applications to both intra- and interorganizational processes of one sort or another, Paquet's pioneering work in Canada (1997, 1999, 2005) drew attention to the need for a country, or a domestic subnational jurisdiction such as a province or city, to foster productive working relationships between sectors.

In contrast to Jacobs' emphasis on distinction and Stanbury's portrayal of strategic differences and the management of such differences, Paquet underlines the need for dialogue, cross-fertilization, and strategic alignment as critical ingredients of competitiveness, productivity, and prosperity. In other words, cooperation between sectors is essential, and while this point is more or less universally accepted today, it was a much more contested notion during the 1990s, particularly in North American and other Anglo-Saxon countries, where there had been a wider ideological gulf between market and state (a remnant, as discussed earlier, of the related Cold War ideological battles pitting state-driven communism against market-based capitalism).

Whereas Jacobs serves as a reminder that each sector within the Boulding triangle has a unique purpose (which in turn shapes how individuals and organizations behave within each sector), Paquet's focus on the systemic governance challenges of coordination and adaptive performance capacities embraces a much greater degree of fluidity across sectors as virtuous. Moreover, although this book's emphasis is primarily on the interactions between business and government, the Boulding triangle is also a useful reminder that such interaction is often influenced by the presence and mobilization of the civic or third sector. Non-profit organizations, non-governmental organizations, and less formalized social movements (many of them are virtual in formation) all occupy an important dimension of governance in the industrialized world.

Globalization and technological innovation heighten the importance of strategically aligning both the outer and the inner boundaries of the Boulding triangle as a depiction of jurisdictional governance. Only the collective learning of a system as a whole can therefore suffice. Indeed, in this first decade of the twenty-first century, the term "governance" has become something akin to a global ideology of how countries (as well as jurisdictions both within and among them) must organize themselves in order to succeed. Mintzberg (1996) made this point with respect to spheres of management and organization (emphasizing sectoral distinctions and the allocation of specific functions to each sector), whereas Fukuyama (2004) frames the governance challenge as one that is more encompassing of distinct but also aligned institutional spheres that collectively determine a country's ability to steer itself in an increasingly turbulent environment.

With its emphasis on interdependence and relational complexity, the Boulding triangle and Paquet's portrayals of governance are well aligned with, and make important use of, stakeholder theory. For instance, the commonly used application of the term "stakeholder" is in the realm of corporate governance — embedding the private firm within a Boulding triangle–like set of partnerships and obligations. The OECD (2004) definition of corporate governance — perhaps the closest example of a global consensus across considerably different cultural and geographical viewpoints — thereby includes an explicit recognition of such stakeholder ties alongside shareholder interests as a basis of optimal corporate behaviour.

At the same time, the applicability of corporate governance as a composite of shareholder and stakeholder relationships extends beyond the marketplace. In the public sector, for example, crown corporations, regulatory agencies, and traditional departments reorganizing themselves according to performance-based management principles all carry corporate governance challenges. A steadily increasing reliance on non-profit structures, both within civil society and as hybrid entities across private and public interests (e.g., airport authorities, discussed in chapter 1), also entails corporate governance choices, even as invocation of the term "corporate" may or may not carry from one sectoral setting to another.

Therefore, in a manner fashioned on Paquet's co-evolutionary perspective, the OECD goes further in recognizing corporate governance as a systemic and collective challenge for a jurisdiction as a whole and, indeed, as foundational for global prosperity (Witherall 2000). Aside from well-performing governance structures within the market sector (or within any sector for that matter), the legal and political frameworks of any jurisdiction must be suitable for fair and productive economic initiatives to form.

TRANSCENDING NATIONAL BOUNDARIES

The Boulding triangle, the policy arena, and the positive and negative mixing of commercial and guardian syndromes all depict in some fashion the specific boundaries of a governance jurisdiction or system — most typically a country. Yet, in today's globalizing world, national governance systems are closely intertwined with forces transcending any one nation. For a small-population, trade-dependent, and culturally diverse country such as Canada, this truism could not be more pronounced.

In the first decade of the twenty-first century, technology and security rival trade and investment as the predominant forces of globalization. As during the aftermath of World War II, when the parameters of free trade and open borders were forged, today the United States lies at the heart of this shift and the resulting impacts on globalization generally and on Canadian governance specifically. Both are of interest in this book, since understanding business-government relations in Canada today requires sensitivity to the interplay among domestic, continental, and global levels.

The terrorist attacks of September 2001 are an important inflection point — although US skepticism toward multilateralism and more integrative forms of political authority had already become evident upon President Bush's 2000 electoral victory. Quite aside from antiterrorist actions that have since defined the Bush presidency, for many observers US insularity first emerged under the Bush administration with rejection of the Kyoto Accord and has continued since.

Such a trend was similarly evident in 2005 when the US government resisted pressure from most other countries, including European allies, to create a more multilateral venue for administering the technical nucleus of the Internet. Widening unease about offshore outsourcing and the divisive nexus between border security and largely Hispanic immigration flows further underscore this refocusing of American energy away from building a global order toward one of refurbishing perceived domestic weaknesses.

The implications of this US shift for governance cultures and business-government relations (in both the United States and elsewhere) are illustrated by the 2005 port security scandal involving a Dubai-based company. The entity, Dubai Ports World, fresh from a takeover of the port management operations of the British multinational, faced howls of protest in the US Congress, across the political spectrum, largely due to its Middle Eastern origins. The fact that several of the 9/11 hijackers had transited through Dubai (a city-state of the United Arab Emirates) certainly did not help the public relations aspect of the issue.

Nonetheless, quite aside from the politics of American–Middle Eastern relations is an equally telling aspect of the crisis: namely, the willingness of the US federal government (at least the executive branch, including defence and security agencies) to cede key portions of the country's commercially driven ports to a government-owned entity from a foreign jurisdiction. Prior to 9/11, such a transaction would likely have received criticism on the ground of unfair competition via state subsidization. In

2005, US government agencies initially endorsed the deal largely since government control was viewed as a plus (the United Arab Emirates has been a silent but staunch ally in US-led antiterrorism efforts in the region).

Such an example is indicative of a growing acceptance of a range of governance models and mixes of private and public involvements. Today Airbus is firmly established as Boeing's chief "commercial" rival, despite its state-backed origins, and the same logic is replaying itself in the realm of Internet search engines as European governments have banded together to fund what is hoped to be a European equivalent capable of quelling Google's dominance of virtual searches (and by extension the dominance of English and an American company).

This prospect of a diminishing US determination to promote market structures and private business models over state involvements externally is also accompanied by the need for closer industry-government alignment and collaboration at home. The nexus between security and technology (and related military endeavours) drives an embracing of public-private collaboration to a degree that would have been harshly rejected by Republicans in decades past. The main point here is not to suggest that the United States has abandoned the merits of market competition and private enterprise in favour of wider public sector involvements but that it is joining much of the rest of the world in becoming more pragmatic about where lines are drawn between the two spheres.

As elsewhere, moreover, the United States has confronted its own difficulties in recent years in terms of less appropriate interactions between industry and government: the corporate governance scandals beginning with Enron and WorldComm, lobbying scandals such as those involving Jack Abramoff, corporate bribery and government corruption scandals involving US federal government procurement officials and employees of Boeing, and widening tensions between industry and government involving consumer information holdings and the sharing of such information between the private and public sectors.

In this first decade of the twenty-first century, the US experience in terms of business-government relations is very indicative of a world of countries that are at once embracing capitalism and seeking tailored versions of it to meet domestic realities and interests. While the United States remains the lone military superpower, it is becoming less exceptional as an ideological poster child and more normal as an economic and political competitor, itself struggling to promote domestic interests and address domestic insecurities.

The consequences for Canada are profound, and a central premise of this book is that it is impossible to examine business-government relations in Canada without placing them in a Canada-US context. There are two reasons for such a claim. First, as argued above, the US experience is important in shaping globalization and the actions and governance choices of all countries. Second, many specific competitive choices and policy challenges within the Canadian marketplace and political system are directly intertwined with continental realities, be they integrative processes or degrees of separation between both countries.

As a case in point, Canadian industry is increasingly focused on continental markets, in terms of not only trade access but also market structure. Sectors such as airlines, financial services, and telecommunications all involve increasingly cross-border market patterns that are at odds with domestic competition rules and regulatory regimes. Similarly, the Canadian federal government has closely modelled its post-9/11 responses after those of the United States, expanding domestic security capabilities and prioritizing border security and those issues of most concern to US authorities. The politics of such bilateral convergence became more pronounced following Canada's 2006 federal election, which saw a Conservative government come to power on a platform not unlike that of the new Republicanism south of the border that seeks to blend traditional skepticism of state action with an expansion of government authority in the limited realms of military defence and domestic security.

The second major theme permeating much of this book, also intertwined with Canada-US relations in various manners, is the rising importance of information and communications technologies and broadband infrastructure. The emergence of digital governance processes both within and across the public and private sectors can be examined across all three of the relational templates reviewed.

Here too the United States is an important reference point for Canada, not only in terms of border management and bilateral relations but also in terms of what Canada can learn from the security-technology nexus and its impacts on business-government relations. The United States is making more visible interrelationships between industry and government, which are central to governance in an information age. Recent debates in the United States pertaining to the Patriot Act and government wiretapping and data-mining programs that rely on industry participation are no less important in Canada. They are less publicly probed, however, and thus more subversive. It is telling in this regard that the limited examples of politicized incidents in Canada, such as the Arar affair and privacy concerns involving contracts between Canadian-based subsidiaries of US companies and public data holdings in BC provincial authorities, are intertwined with American involvements of one sort or another.[4]

What is clear, however, from domestic events in the United States is that along with a new cosiness between industry and government also comes the potential for tension and conflict. The American federal government's legal proceedings against Google over access to online search records are a case in point. Similarly, the prosecution of a leading data-processing company, Choice Point, for breaches of privacy is indicative of a toughening of state and federal regulations over private industry that, while many observers in the United States continue to view as insufficient, is nonetheless more aggressive than the more voluntary regulatory and disclosure regimes in Canada.

In both countries, new sectoral and intergovernmental tensions have arisen over models of broadband infrastructure deployment and the emergence of wireless cities, first in the United States and now in Canada. Such debates centre on whether Internet access is best left to markets or to some form of public good provisioning, and it provides a useful illustration of how different industries lobby governments on a single issue from a variety of self-interest–based vantage points. Indeed, both countries are reviewing their telecommunications apparatus (and the very essence of this term in a digital world) at a time when North America is beginning to lose ground to other parts of the world in broadband penetration and wireless and cell phone usage specifically.

In sum, these interrelated themes of continental governance and digital connectivity provide much of the context in this book, which leads to the selection of specific policy and strategy issues examined below. I have chosen these themes not only because they are interesting and topical but also because they are tremendously consequential to the specific actions of companies and governments as well as the collective fortunes of countries and continents in the first part of the twenty-first century.

THE STORYLINE IN BRIEF

The purpose of each chapter is not to assess which of the three aforementioned templates of business-government relations is more or less useful. Although perhaps in unequal proportions, each one holds some resonance for understanding how business and government are dealing and working with one another in Canada today. Instead, each chapter presents a specific thematic topic that is proving instrumental in shaping business-government relations in terms of their independence, their influencing abilities on one another, or their interdependence and collaborative capacities.

Chapter 1 begins with corporate governance, a term traditionally denoting the conduct and accountability of companies but with increasing resonance in the public sector. Accordingly, a dichotomy of shareholder and stakeholder governance is adopted as a basis for understanding the search for good governance models and practices and how this search is relevant to both private and public enterprise.

Chapter 2 examines lobbying, an important component of the information flows that shape the patterns of influence and learning across sectors. This examination includes the ethical and strategic dimensions of lobbying activity and how these dimensions are changing in light of greater information sharing and communications and calls for greater transparency and accountability. The scope of lobbying and its specific practices are contrasted across Canada and the United States, thereby comparing the role of lobbyists across the parliamentary and presidential models of democracy and the resulting organization of the policy arena in each setting.

The focus of chapter 3 is the increasing importance of partnerships between industry and government in financing and operating systems that are vital to economic, social, and technological development. The mixtures of public and private interests in shared governance models deployed to both construct and maintain traditional forms of hard infrastructure (e.g., roads and hospitals) as well as less tangible forms of more virtual and service-based infrastructure present numerous challenges in terms of industry-government relations. The need for appropriate sectoral boundaries, the conditions for intersectoral collaboration, and the implications for risks and results in both the public and private realms — as well as between them — are the major topics addressed.

Chapter 4 addresses privacy and security. In a virtual world, how information is both handled within each sector and shared between sectors is an important issue for all individuals and organizations. Here the conflicts between proprietary relationships and personal freedoms and collective needs of national security are intensifying, as are related threats such as cyber-crime and identity theft. Furthermore, while closer collaboration between industry and government is key to safeguarding this infrastructure, new tensions between market and political forces are also emerging over the gathering and sharing of information.

Chapter 5 examines the relationship between the geography of place and the patterns of innovation that shape prosperity: collaborative challenges between all sectors are dramatically more important in a world driven by economic innovation, human mobility, and digital connectivity. Both nationally and locally, the widening acceptance of stakeholder collaboration in order to promote collective competitiveness and performance has led to a focus on dynamic clusters, learning and innovation systems, and the search for recipes for the most creative and supportive communities that together constitute "smartness" in a governance environment that is at once globalizing and localizing.

Drawing on Silicon Valley as an important reference point, I consider proximity as a driver of innovation as well as countervailing currents of globalization and virtualization that have altered traditional notions of place and intellectual property. I then examine the geography of Canada's innovation and the local governance capacities in cities and communities. I also consider the manner in which the federalist architecture of Canada's public sector may be out of step with the increasingly global and local dimensions of market activity.

Together these five storylines depict critical contours of business and government interactions in a contemporary and increasingly digital environment—within which governance systems, as well as organizations, compete. As with any country, then, Canada's prospects for future success depend on the ability of business and government to respect one another's differences while also aligning their resources and competencies when shared interests present themselves.

In contrast to Jacobs' monstrous hybrids, the conclusion of this book makes the case for the necessity of virtuous hybrids in moving forward. It also sketches out the main contours of Canada's adaptive challenge in order to facilitate the formation and successful performance of such hybrids, a challenge that calls for political leadership and the broadest possible degree of social learning. An informed and engaged public, wearing multiple hats (e.g., voter, shareholder, employee, activist, etc.), is the ultimate arbitrator of both sectoral and collective performance.

CHAPTER ONE

CORPORATE GOVERNANCE

This chapter introduces the topic of corporate governance as increasingly uniting rather than separating business and government in terms of their organization and conduct. Typically thought of in the realm of a private company, corporate governance denotes the mechanisms for accountability and alignment enjoining corporate management, shareholders, and stakeholders. Increasingly, however, similar terminology is found in the public sector as governments strive to rebalance traditional political control and more innovative governance models predicated on bettering performance.

While fundamental differences between each sector remain, and must be understood as such, corporate governance as a strategic balance between the competing objectives of conformance and performance denotes an increasingly shared challenge for business and government. Such a challenge calls for at least a partial transcending of sectoral boundaries in order to foster mutual awareness, collective learning, and strong performance capacities for a jurisdiction as a whole.

INFORMATION AND COORDINATION

Information is the foundation for governance in any context, be it organizational, sectoral (e.g., the marketplace or the state), or jurisdictional (e.g., a city or country). The emergence of governance as something of a unifying culture across sectors and cultures reflects the widening availability and production of information on the one hand and heightened competition for quick and effective usage of information on the other.

Across business and government, approaches to managing information flows are often contrasted: hierarchies as the basis of bureaucratic control in the public realm (a basis for Jacobs' guardian syndrome) and competition and networks in the private realm (more consistent with the commercial behavioural syndrome). Yet such distinctions can also be fluid. For instance, after World War II, hierarchical-based bureaucratic management principles were in good currency in industry as much as in government, whereas the more recent rise of new public management seeks greater usages of networks and competitive solutions within government. Much of the present contrast between rigid hierarchy and flexible networks has to do with how people are managed within organizations, but an equally important dimension of this governance dichotomy is the availability of information and the relative degree of secrecy and propriety deemed suitable for a particular organizational context.

Throughout much of the twentieth century, across both guardian enterprises (e.g., the military) and commercial entities (e.g., IBM in its early mainframe days with its self-titled corporate motto, "big blue"), scarce information flows tended to be dominated by limited sets of organizations with the wherewithal to capture the information and translate it into specific policies and strategies. Public and private sector entities alike became inward, often benefiting from economies of scale as big proved better — so long as the external environment remained relatively stable (as was the case in the "thirty glorious years" of largely uninterrupted economic expansion that followed World War II in much of the Western world — viewed by some as a not-so-glorious period that enshrined high government-spending levels now difficult to contain[1]).

Today this old paradigm has long since given way to global competitiveness pressures and what some have termed "the age of transparency" (Tapscott and Ticoll 2003). Innovation is often viewed as the purview of small start-ups (at times created within larger corporate structures seeking to escape bureaucratic rigidness and facilitate flexibility). The collaborative and mobile work culture of Silicon Valley is put forth as the most promising ecology of shared information and learning externalities, forcing all organizations to become vigilantly insecure and outward in orientation. In this new context, prosperity has come to resemble a more volatile path of "creative destructionism," to borrow the phrasing of a prominent twentieth-century political economist, Joseph Schumpeter (1947).

Yet a continuing need for accountability and the rising demands for more of it from all types of organizations have created new governance dilemmas. Unfettered competitive instincts and weak controls can fuel corporate scandals such as those of Enron and Nortel. Yet an excessive shift to control or guardian functions risks stifling innovation and risk taking. Similar dilemmas face government organizations: creativity can often be viewed as lax by those seeking clarity and control, while taken to an extreme this control orientation reinforces a bureaucratic, risk-averse mentality that embeds bureaucratic structures (often viewed as wasteful and unresponsive). Resolving these dilemmas requires an artful governance balance that, while not identical across the private and public realms, also carries similarities across and synergies among them.

SHAREHOLDER AND STAKEHOLDER RELATIONS

In recent times, there has been an important debate with respect to corporate governance in the private sector and the appropriate roles, objectives, and accountability frameworks for businesses. Broadly stated, two schools of thought influence this debate: shareholder value on the one hand and stakeholder value on the other.

The notion of shareholder value is both more straightforward and more readily accepted (particularly in North America) as the appropriate prism for gauging corporate behaviour and performance. Companies focus on profitability, return on investment, and widely recognized metrics of value creation such as share price. In this focus, the most fundamental and overriding accountability relationship is between owners of capital (investors) and managers.

By contrast, stakeholder value places the company within a wider set of accountability relationships that should ideally be both recognized and measured: examples include employees, communities, research partners, and clients. Investing in these relationships is the basis of sustaining capacities for performance, particularly through changing circumstances. Pursuing stakeholder value is complicated by the plurality of stakeholder relationships that exist and by disagreement over what sort of balance should be struck between shareholder and stakeholder considerations.

This debate carries overtones of Jacobs' contrast between commercial and guardian syndromes, and defenders of a more purely shareholder-driven model of governance for private enterprise would be quick to underscore the commercial logic of linking risk, private investment, and direct lines of accountability between investors and managers. Within the limits of the law (determined by guardians), institutionalizing the generation and distribution of shareholder wealth should be business's sole purpose.

In the United States, some observers are even prepared to extend this logic to the most extreme example, such as Enron. While many have viewed it as a failure of corporate governance, others have suggested that Enron's illegal activities (including accounting fraud and misinformation) directly resulted in convictions against the company's top managers, the failure of the multinational accounting firm duplicitous in the company's schemes, and the disappearance of most shareholder value associated with this former energy giant. How could one possibly demand greater accountability for inappropriate action?

To some degree, the partial merit of such a viewpoint explains the reluctance in the United States to radically overhaul market structures and practices—for fear of tempering the entrepreneurial spirit that is viewed as the driver of wealth creation in a free-enterprise system. Instead, the emphasis has been on bolstering the guardians of market behaviour, such as state and federal oversight bodies (at the federal level, the powers of the Securities and Exchange Commission have been expanded, and a new independent body has been established under federal purview to oversee the accounting profession).

Some commentators even argue that the dubious conduct of business in cases such as Enron and WorldComm has empowered high-profile guardians such as New York State Attorney General Eliot Spitzer, who has led several high-profile investigations of corporate misbehaviour in several leading American industries, including computer manufacturing, insurance, entertainment, and securities trading. In perhaps the most notable of his cases, Spitzer's pursuit of Wall Street firms exposed inherent conflicts of interest between the stock research and endorsement functions of brokerage housing, leading to more than $1.5 billion of fines levied (including a $100 million payment by Merrill Lynch alone) and significant changes to industry practices and regulations.

Nevertheless, such corrective measures stemming from the logic of guardians overseeing the otherwise unfettered activities of commercial actors are insufficient. Equally important are the failures of governance mechanisms within the market sphere itself. In the most spectacular US example, Enron, such failures fuelled not only the widespread and dramatic financial losses of millions of Enron investors (including employees whose pension funds were wiped away) but also the collateral damage to other industries (as investor confidence stagnated) and other sectors, such as governments and individual consumers facing rising energy bills and new supply challenges due to the dubious activities of Enron management.

Chief among these failures is the board of directors, the body supposedly convened as the representatives of shareholders to watch over management and ensure that the interests of investors are taken into account. In essence, management serves as the agent of the principals or the owners (i.e., shareholders), a key indirect aspect of marketplace accountability, since the individual shareholder (unless an institution yielding considerable clout) is unlikely to possess the information and the means to effectively scrutinize corporate activity. This separation of powers is akin in some respects to the ideal role of parliamentarians in their representation of voters in the public sector realm.

In the case of Enron and many other such examples (including Nortel in Canada), the board of directors proved impotent due primarily to (1) a lack of independence from management, in large part because of the excessive influence of corporate executives in appointing board members, including the chairperson, and (2) conflicts from shared as opposed to separate interests with management as short-term price became the defining prism of corporate activity (often with board members themselves holding shares) as opposed to long-term growth and sustainability.

Although this latter term may be invoked in a strictly financial or shareholder value sense (i.e., viewing investment returns over a longer time horizon), invocation of the term "sustainability" also conjures up the notion of stakeholder involvement for companies as they balance their multiple obligations not only to investors-shareholders but also to other groups impacted by corporate operations, such as employees, communities, governments, and other civic and societal partners, such as research entities and collaborative undertakings of one sort or another.

Although some business theorists view a focus on anything other than profit as misguided from a commercial perspective, there is an equally influential contingent of business advocates that stresses the importance of long-term relationship building to business success (Kennedy 2000; Miles and Roy 2001). Time is a particularly contentious variable here, with advocates of shareholder value often more focused on short-term proxies such as quarterly earnings and share price, whereas those preferring stakeholder balance and sustainability-oriented outlooks often invoke longer time horizons, arguing that great companies can only be judged as such after several years, if not decades, of proven success (Collins 1994, 2001).[2]

The ecological context of business operations is a closely related aspect cutting across many of these stakeholder ties (also introducing new ones such as environmental groups more hostile to corporate objectives). Accordingly, much of today's focus on corporate social responsibility (CSR), as well as the steadily expanding influence of ethical investment funds (seeking to reward corporate performance on CSR-type activities as well as financial results: i.e., multiple dimensions of a balanced scorecard), stems from environmental processes such as roundtables that emerged in the 1990s following the high-profile, UN-sponsored Earth Summit in Rio de Janeiro in 1992.

The complexities of sustainable development and the intermixing of industrial production and environmental resources have led some leading proponents of ecosensitive business models to either implicitly or directly counter Jacobs' dichotomy of commercial and guardian orientations. One such example is Paul Hawken (1993), who viewed Jacobs' approach as dangerously limiting, placing the environmental onus firmly on guardians (to craft and enforce rules and punish misdeeds) in an era when multinational corporations and business interests carry enormous resources and influence themselves.

Hawken's preference for a sustainability compact encompassing all sectors in a progressive and productive hybrid model find echoes today in Al Gore's global campaign for a greening of industry in response to global warming. Similar influences underpin the reforestation policies of lumber companies engaged in environmental roundtables, attempting to balance short-term economic opportunity with a longer-term nurturing of a potentially renewable resource.

Even with some consensus on the importance of addressing environmental issues, the contrasting assessments of Hawken and Jacobs underline the absence of any consensus on the sectoral boundaries appropriate for any solutions, much less on corporate governance practices to balance shareholder and stakeholder considerations (the latter an inherently contested notion). Despite corporate governance reforms to refurbish the board as an independent mechanism to oversee management on behalf of shareholders (most predominant among them a focus on independent directors and a non-executive chair), board membership remains largely shareholder and financial in orientation. What has emerged is something akin to a global consensus — under the auspices of the OECD guidelines on corporate governance, that stakeholder interests should be accounted for — with little specific guidance on the appropriate means to reach such a consensus.

Nonetheless, the rising tide of stakeholder relations reflects more than knee-jerk reactions to crises; it is intertwined with the expansion of markets and the corresponding heightened influence of private corporations. The growing power (and by extension impacts and responsibilities) of corporations in today's globalizing environment, coupled with heightened and more knowledgeable classes of investors, means that a return to cozy, shielded working relationships involving executive managers and their board counterparts appears unlikely. An increasingly diverse set of both collaborative and competitive interests can be expected to attempt to shape corporate behaviour, rendering patterns of governance more complex and the management of such patterns more consequential.

In 2006, for instance, Microsoft announced on its corporate website that it had commissioned a study of its external stakeholder relationships to better navigate what is today often characterized as a corporate ecosystem of various actors and interests. Along with its still predominant annual financial report, the world's leading technology company produces an annual report of responsible corporate behaviour, and beyond the company's actions the evolution of Microsoft founder Bill Gates from chief executive to a global advocate of health and antipoverty strategies further demonstrates the widening role of business interests in non-commercial matters.

The Guardian's Response: Exhortation or Regulation?
From the government's perspective, these corporate governance challenges raise two interrelated responses. First, from a

guardian perspective, public sector authorities carry certain regulatory obligations in terms of enforcing rules and/or promoting specific governance practices within the marketplace. At the most basic level, the judicial system is a case in point, upholding the legal dimensions of commercial exchange and contractual duties that are major aspects of a well-functioning corporate governance environment. Beyond legal enforcement and redress, however, the government can choose to largely empower private companies to self-monitor their behaviour, or it can empower specific institutions such as professional bodies and stock markets to administer ethical guidelines and rules beyond basic legal standards and requirements. In Canada, such powers reside across a diverse set of actors, including predominantly provincial regulatory authorities for investing and stock markets, the stock market authorities themselves (notably, the Toronto Stock Exchange [TSX], by far the country's largest venue of publicly traded companies), the Canadian Institute of Chartered Accountants (overseeing the auditing profession), and indirectly numerous federal agencies with regulatory and law enforcement powers.

In the aftermath of scandals such as Enron, WorldComm, and Nortel, the TSX took the lead in concert with several other industry groups in developing stricter governance codes for listed companies. The results of such actions have not been negligible in fostering what the TSX described as a stronger governance culture for companies and for the country as a whole. Today there are stricter rules in place for companies listed on the TSX, the impacts of which are visible on any corporate website. More balanced board representation (with a separation of chief executive and board chair and the vesting of the latter in a non-executive party), greater independence for auditing committees, and stricter guidelines for information disclosure have become norms of market activity that were exceptions less than a decade ago.

For industry leaders, despite the negative impacts of scandals such as the Nortel collapse, Canada is well served by a light-handed approach that relies on tough guardians in extreme cases but also on more sensitized commercial behaviour in the mainstream. As the head of the Canadian Council of Chief Executives puts it,

> The Council's emphasis on voluntary action has been portrayed by some people as a "laissez-faire" attitude, a go slow approach that is out of touch with today's market realities. It is true that the Council favours a principles-based rather than rules-based approach to improving governance practises. But that is because we believe that comprehensive guidelines, built on a solid legal and regulatory foundation and backed up by mandatory disclosure, are in fact a more effective way to improve the norms of acceptable behaviour and prevent abuses of public trust than any approach that relies excessively on precise but narrow rules.[3]

By the same token, however, Canada has often been portrayed as more reticent in pursuing criminal charges against corporate offences, preferring the softer, more indirect hand of self-regulation and competitive pressures from within the marketplace (Fasken/Martineau 2002). Although not of identical proportions, a cursory comparison of Enron and Nortel underlines this point. In the former case, several key executives have been criminally convicted, while numerous other players have either escaped prosecution or lessened their charges by virtue of negotiated plea bargains with federal prosecutors.

By contrast, no criminal charges have been pursued against former Nortel executives in Canada, although several investor-initiated legal suits have been settled by the corporation in recent years. Nortel has also been the recipient of a grand jury subpoena from US judicial authorities in Texas, an investigation with which it has claimed to be fully complying. Indeed, no doubt due to the amplitude of scandals and investor loss and outrage (investors who are also voters), the US response, led by a Republican administration generally characterized as pro-business, was swift and far more sweeping than anything undertaken in Canada: "Among other measures, the 2002 Sarbanes-Oxley Act, motivated by the Enron collapse and other scandals, required companies to set up comprehensive internal controls and established a new federal board to oversee auditors. It also demanded that top executives sign off on their companies' financial statements—holding them personally liable if it was later found that someone else had cooked the books."[4]

Partly stung by criticisms portraying Canada as weak on white-collar crime, the federal government created a new unit of the RCMP in 2003 to focus on corporate investigations (including Nortel, with investigations ongoing during the first half of 2006). After three years of operation, however, this unit has laid no charges in any private sector investigation, leading to widening questions about both the resolve and the capacity of Canadian authorities to pursue alleged failures of corporate governance.

Much of corporate governance is more subtle, however, involving the millions upon millions of minute decisions made every day by companies, their managers, and representatives of shareholders and stakeholders. For this reason, authorities such as the TSX often invoke the "culture" of governance as more than enforcement (as per the passage above).

It bears noting that this cultural approach underscores the need for hybrid mechanisms that transcend Jacobs' ideally separate syndromes—since an accepted attribute of commercial actors is to shun authority and take risks (implying that it may not be all that unusual for governance failures to occur). At the same time, however, effective corporate governance regimes (even as they serve all companies collectively) require not only some measure of self-policing by companies (at times a derivative of competition) but also the existence of guardian functions within a company's governance architecture (notably the board).

CORPORATE GOVERNANCE IN GOVERNMENT

The complexities of corporate governance underscore Jacobs' depiction of the need for separate yet complementary authority from commercial and guardian perspectives: competition and strong and effective shareholder governance mechanisms are essential, but so are serious guardian capacities with the willingness and authority to investigate and punish wrongdoing as necessary. Conversely, widening calls for stakeholder dimensions of corporate governance suggest a mixing of commercial and guardian functions that concerned Jacobs (i.e., the potential for the formation of monstrous hybrids), but this mixing has been viewed as both inevitable and appropriate by others.

To understand how and why corporate governance has become more common in the public sector realm, it is useful to begin with an association of the "stakeholder" orientation as one more commonly invoked in government. Operating in the public interest, the absence of a single, linear objective such as financial profitability and economic surplus — coupled with the inherently contested notion of the public interest itself — invariably translates into governments responding to multiple groups (i.e., stakeholders) laying claims to matters of public interest. It is not surprising, then, that skeptics of the notion of stakeholder governance for companies view it as an inappropriate fusion of commercial and guardian roles or, to make the point more crassly, as forcing business to behave more like government.

Increasingly, however, there is a similar countermovement emerging from pressures on government to behave more like business (Eggers 2005). Partly tied to the ideologies of certain governments, partly rooted in the business-inspired principles of certain reform streams of the new public management philosophy, and partly due to the widening space for collaborative public-private activities, corporate governance is likewise being imported into the public sector realm (Ehrenworth 2003).

The formalities of democratic governance are more naturally welcoming of the language of stakeholders than that of shareholders (although, in the late 1990s, a former trade minister of a centralist Liberal government publicly referred to Canada as a great "corporation" and its citizens as "shareholders"). Yet similarities of coordinating decisions and strategies in a performance-driven manner have resulted in traditionally corporate-based mechanisms—boards in particular (or close variants such as advisory bodies)—as means of attempting to improve the governance and performance of public sector entities.

Although boards have often been used for crown corporations (government-owned but arm's-length agencies such as Canada Post), their usage has extended gradually into the core of the public service. Often the objective is to create stronger and more independent managerial oversight of public corporations than traditional political forums have been able to achieve. The Canada Revenue Agency is a case in point, where a board of management oversees the operational aspects of the tax agency, complementing political oversight responsibilities that remain vested in the minister (who, in turn, must account to Parliament for the overall conduct of the agency and any specific matters raised by elected officials on behalf of the public).

The most recent reforms in Canada, focused on more transparent and merit-based appointments to such boards—especially those of traditional bodies such as crown corporations—underscore the extension of a governance culture today that features distinct circumstances but increasingly common conduct with respect to performance and accountability principles that apply across both the marketplace and the state. Such commonalities have also led to non-profit alternatives as a means of aligning corporate governance practices within areas involving a public interest. Perhaps the most prominent examples in Canada are those bodies created to administer the conduct of airport authorities and air travel security. The latter, NAV Canada, is self-described on its website as a private sector, non-share capital corporation financed through publicly traded debt, a model that defies simplistic categorization as private or public (and, not surprisingly, leads to many media references to the body as simply privatization).

The role of government, however, remains central since it is hardly conceivable that political accountability for safe handling of air trafficking could be completely diverged away from elected governments (indeed, in the aftermath of 9/11, the US federal government renationalized most aspects of airport security that had been outsourced to the private sector). NAV Canada's success as a governance hybrid has been to balance its relationships to both guardian and commercial stakeholders, and in doing so it has adapted a specific model of board governance to meet these particular needs.

Rather than shareholders, the company has four members:

- the Government of Canada,
- the Air Transport Association of Canada (representing air carriers),
- the Canadian Business Aviation Association (representing business and general aviation), and
- the NAV Canada Bargaining Agents Association (repre-senting employee bargaining agents).

These members appoint ten individuals to NAV CANADA's board of directors:

- air carriers — four,
- general and business aviation — one,
- federal government — three, and
- bargaining agents — two.

These ten directors then elect four independent directors, and the board appoints the president and chief executive officer to form the corporation's board of fifteen directors. This structure ensures that the board knows the views of all the key stakeholders. It also makes certain that the interests of individual stakeholders do not predominate, since no member can elect a majority of directors.[5]

With respect to airport facilities on the ground, privatization was considered by many governments across North America in order to upgrade airport facilities in a more competitive, efficient, and responsive fashion regarded as beyond the capabilities of direct government authority. While many US airports were privatized, ideological concerns over market control around an asset regarded as a key element of public infrastructure led to the search for a more politically palatable alternative, one that would nonetheless combine private sector flexibility and performance with a more collective form of accountability.

Having been a major issue in the 1993 federal election campaign, abandonment of the proposed privatization of Pearson International Airport would lead to the creation of local airport authorities, which now operate in most major Canadian cities. From a corporate governance perspective, the authorities represent a stakeholder model of corporate governance, as illustrated by the case of the Calgary Airport Authority:

> The corporate governance processes of The Authority are structured to promote the purposes and business of The Authority as set forth in the Regional Airports Authorities Act (Alberta) and the Canada Lease. Pursuant to The Authority's Articles of Incorporation, the following four bodies appoint Directors to the Board:
>> The Long-Range Planning Committee of the Calgary Chamber of Commerce, which appoints 11 Board members;
>> The Corporation of the City of Calgary, which appoints three Board members;
>> The Government of Canada, which appoints two Board members; and
>> The Municipal District of Rocky View, which appoints one Board member.[6]

In such a model, the purpose of the board is not primarily to represent shareholders at large (since the only meaningful shareholder is ultimately the crown) but to represent key interests impacted by and strategically tied to airport infrastructure. Although perhaps it is not monstrous (Jacobs' extremity), critics of such a hybrid approach to state-based corporate governance arise from two competing vantage points. First, proponents of more outright privatization suggest that the absence of truly private ownership dulls the incentives of board members to foster financial probity and efficiency-minded behaviour: without the pressures and incentives of market competition, the board is more likely to support wider investments and thus higher costs that are passed along, in the case of airport authorities, to travellers. Second, skeptics from the opposite direction often concur with the problem of higher fees arising from what amounts to near-monopolistic control over a public asset, but their main concern is the lack of direct public oversight in managing such decisions (as illustrated above, private sector interests are predominant).

As foreshadowed by the implicit debates between Jacobs, Hawken, and others, these types of governance hybrids are becoming more common, particularly with respect to the construction and maintenance of new infrastructure (a topic of chapter 3). The extended usage of board mechanisms across both purely shareholder and more hybrid, stakeholder-based governance models reflects widening demands for accountability that balance probity and performance across a spectrum of profitability in the realm of the market and public purpose within that of the state. Accordingly, the language of corporate governance is becoming a regular feature in business and government as enterprises in both sectors seek an appropriate mix of control and oversight on the one hand and flexibility and empowerment on the other.

GOVERNANCE FOR CONFORMANCE AND PERFORMANCE

There are two simultaneous lessons to be derived from a critical governance failure such as that of Enron, both of which highlight the importance of boundaries and balances across both organizational and sectoral governance systems. The first and foremost lesson is that Enron executives were proven to have broken the law and punished accordingly (the company's former chief executive and chairman of the board—the combination being a corporate governance red flag—would succumb to a heart attack before prison sentencing began following his conviction). The lesson here is that a competitive and well-functioning market of demonstrated fairness and legitimacy for all potential managers and owners/investors (i.e., underpinning the commercial syndrome) requires strong offsetting public sector mechanisms of oversight and enforcement (i.e., the guardians). With greed a natural attribute of market-driven behaviour, and inherent in such behaviour the taking of risks, a strong measure of policing and enforcement is essential to ensure that the clearest, most fundamental legal boundaries of what is acceptable are respected.

Yet the second lesson from Enron's spectacular rise and fall is the importance of achieving an artful governance balance across all stakeholders if a corporate venture is to sustain its growth and success. Many of the more subtle but nonetheless consequential failures of governance at Enron involved a board of directors narrowly fixated on profitability and shareholder value (neglecting not only fiduciary duties to ensure the legitimacy of such results but also their strategic role in probing whether or not the company was exercising due care and respect for its clients, employees, supporting communities, and other stakeholders affected by its rising prominence).

While the criminality and tremendous financial implications of Enron's collapse have accentuated the legal categorizations of right and wrong (not only for government-prosecuted executives but also for many former directors facing legal action from disgruntled investors), just as important are the lessons of transparent and inclusive forms of engagement between various stakeholders comprising a company's corporate governance system.

Here the notion of balance applies not only as a dichotomy of contrasting market and state actions (underpinned by unique commercial and guardian behaviour) but also as a necessary attribute of good governance within each sector, in this case within the marketplace and for-profit corporate structures. Here it is worth reinvoking the sustainability message offered by Jim Collins about what makes companies great: balance between what are essentially commercial and guardian-type roles within the company as well as an ongoing strategic dialogue between key stakeholders both inside and outside the corporation.

In his useful study of corporate governance in Canada and elsewhere, Mel Gill (2002) puts forward the following governance typology that adopts the OECD's usage of stakeholders (whereas here the shareholder is but one form of stakeholder) and maps out three basic questions that good governance must address. Governance is the structures, traditions, and processes of leadership and stewardship that

- assign power;
- define roles, responsibilities, and relationships;
- govern communications with stakeholders; and
- ensure accountability (from which legitimacy is derived).

The three basic questions are

- Who has influence?
- Who makes decisions?
- How are decision makers held to account?

Gill further clarifies the differences between governance and management, asserting that while the former is the framework for asking such questions of influence, decision-making power, and accountability, the latter entails implementation and execution within such a framework. The following comparison, presented by Gill, illustrates both realms, which invariably intersect as organizations adapt to a dynamic socioeconomic, political, and technological environment.

Good Governance: Providing a Framework

- Vision/values
- Destinations/outcomes
- Resources/inputs
- Monitoring
- Accountability to owners/stakeholders

Good Management: Implementing within Framework

- Piloting/steering/driving
- Knowing: maps/resources/conditions
- Selecting course from alternative routes
- Ensuring efficient use of resources and good organizational maintenance
- Assessing progress and conditions
- Reporting (to board/crew/passengers)

Gill concludes by calling for a made-in-Canada approach that augments the enforcement rules of public sector guardians (including a Canadian version of the US Securities and Exchange Commission) while seeking an ethos of stakeholder accountability for companies themselves. He further underscores the importance of the transnational environment to align Canadian practices with international standards, such as those put forth by the OECD.

The challenge for companies in building on such templates is not to adhere to them, however sound they may be, but to foster an integrative and open mindset driven by an agenda of learning and constant adaptation. Here the notion of "enterprise governance" has been put forth as a dynamically evolving rubric of two dimensions — *conformance* and *performance* — that must constantly be in balance (International Federation of Accountants 2004). While conformance asks whether appropriate checks and balances are in place across shareholder and stakeholder relationships, performance seeks to leverage these networks into forward-looking capacities for strategizing successfully.

Similar Challenges for Government

For the public sector, the simultaneous importance and the subtleties involved in both boundaries and balances are equally evident and consequential. On the one hand, guardian-laden missions of justice and redistribution—within the parameters of democratic politics and accountability—demand a unique and greater openness to all stakeholders than is appropriate for market activity and thus a greater respect for rules and process. Yet, at the same time, the rising performance demands placed on public enterprise and many new forms of public-private hybrids involving both the efficiency and the effectiveness of service delivery and policy making mean that flexibility and creativity cannot be alien to such structures that otherwise become stifling, unresponsive bureaucracies.

However imperfectly applied and contested, the advent of new public management in the public sector realm seeks to maintain, where appropriate, the boundaries between market and state while enabling the latter to improve its performance abilities through the importation of practices from the former. In a world of constant technological and organizational innovation and change, this intersectoral transfer of means and the often corresponding comparisons made between them are certain to persist.

Yet for some observers, many current problems are indicative of a breakdown of traditional controls brought on by various reforms put forth under the guise of "new public management" and related movements. The result has been a breaking of the traditional "bargain" between elected officials—notably ministers—and public servants: Savoie (2003) specifically laments the loss of traditional boundaries and controls and the resulting erosion of clear lines of accountability.

As Savoie acknowledges, whatever the past strengths of the traditional model of ministerial accountability, one cannot merely reach back and call upon tradition to resolve emerging challenges. The growing imposition of horizontality as not only desirable but also essential—coupled with the dispersal of information and power across an extended public sector of think tanks, academics, special interest groups, and other stakeholders—renders this traditional bargain unworkable in moving forward (Paquet 1997; Bakvis and Juillet 2004; Langford and Roy 2006).

Furthermore, a strong case can be made that present difficulties stem more from reluctance to embrace bolder reforms than from any present deviations from tradition—particularly with respect to the role of public servants and how they are held accountable (Hubbard and Paquet 2005). In many other Westminster-inspired models of parliamentary democracy, senior public servants are truly beginning to be held accountable for results based on their own decisions and authority: performance-based management based less on process rules and responsibilities and more on outcomes and achievements (Aucoin, Smith, and Dinsdale 2004).

In the United Kingdom and New Zealand, for example, many department and agency heads are recruited, appointed, and compensated (and at times removed) on the basis of performance contracts that signify a distinct sphere of autonomy. Nevertheless, accountability of the public servant in charge of managing the agency remains within the confines of policies and political objectives laid out by the government. In Sweden, a similar level of managerial autonomy is complemented by flexibilities that are the basis of a "contractual" and "networked" approach for pursuing aims both vertically and horizontally—as circumstances dictate:

> Owing to the increased need for cooperation between different administrative units, *networked administration* represents an appropriate organizational paradigm for modern administration. The term refers to administration composed of independently managed units that rely on functions and resources provided by other such units or private companies, and form part of permanent and temporary cooperative structures.
>
> Forms of collaboration among administrative units vary according to country and administrative tradition. The Swedish

model of cooperation may be summarized as a *contractual model*. Accordingly, an administrative unit decides for itself whether external services and functions are sufficiently attractive for the unit to use them or pay for this use. (Swedish Agency for Public Management 2004, 2)

Many countries have sought to transform "departments" into "agencies" through significantly enhanced degrees of both autonomy and more explicit managerial roles for public servants. In contrast, the Canadian experience with such reforms — particularly at the federal level — has been timid, due precisely to an unwillingness to move away from a strict and traditional interpretation of ministerial accountability.

The most notable, albeit partial, exception to this trend is the Canada Revenue Agency (CRA), a body that perhaps not coincidentally has realized the greatest progress in establishing online delivery channels that enjoy significant usage among clients.[7] Even here, however, despite an additional margin of both freedom and responsibility for senior management of the revenue agency, the doctrine of full ministerial accountability remains in place, reflecting a form of Canadian compromise between tradition and innovation.

While traditionalists defending the doctrine of ministerial accountability often take solace in the United Kingdom's attachment to Westminster/parliamentary traditions, they will not be comforted by growing calls for reform in that country. In a recent study by a leading British think tank, a recasting of the accountability regime is called for, notable in seeking greater visibility, autonomy, and accountability for public servants in a manner that can be viewed as a nod toward the aforementioned Swedish model: "Government should reform the governance of the civil service as a priority. It needs, in particular, to recast the doctrine of ministerial responsibility....Both ministers and civil servants stand to gain from a greater demarcation of responsibilities. Civil servants will gain new responsibilities and a higher public profile. Ministers will get a professional, better managed, more strategic and outward-looking civil service.

They will also get more support in policy-making" (Lodge and Rogers 2006, 2).

In other words, public servants must become more empowered and more responsible in the managerial realms of administrative design and performance, leaving the broader political tasks of defining the public interest to elected politicians. This distinction stems from the complexity of both policy and operations and the realization that, in the latter realm, public servants are best placed to foster human, organizational, and technological alignment, provided that they have the means to do so. Therefore, in a manner not unlike a private corporation balancing and aligning the roles of managers and the board, partially separate and at times overlapping spheres of influence and duties are likely to denote the new relationship between senior officials appointed to manage and ministers elected on the basis of political vision and a broad set of policy objectives.

While the public sector dynamic of ownership, investment, and return is not akin to that of the marketplace, it is also not foreign to the importance of concepts such as customer service management and responsive stakeholder management. As such, striving for better governance as a means of effectively coordinating and aligning resources, both internally and externally, is a challenge shared by organizations in both sectors.

MOVING BEYOND JACOBS

The more encompassing task for a jurisdiction as a whole is to promote a governance culture that respects the need for both conformance and rules on the one hand and performance-based innovation on the other. Here a strict application of Jacobs' commercial-guardian dichotomy as business and government sectors respectively is overly constraining. There are two reasons.

First, good governance in either sector, for a private or public organization, requires some elements from both the commercial and the guardian orientations. A company's board, for instance, has oversight and control responsibilities on behalf of shareholders, rendering the board guardians—even as they are asked to contribute to the steering of a commercial venture. Similarly, public sector bodies often make use of boards to better balance control and oversight with innovation and a stronger emphasis on performance.

Second, Jacobs' strict boundaries must be transcended because of the need for dialogue across sectors to balance state and market authority and responsibility while also ensuring a cross-fertilization of ideas and competencies across each realm. Whereas scandalous behaviour by businesses will augment the calls for stricter enforcement by the government, more enlightened self-governance efforts, respectful of both shareholder and stakeholder accountabilities, will allow the public sector to be more respectful and supportive of market activity generally while focusing punitive action on a more limited number of cases (action likely to be welcomed by the vast majority of companies striving to balance their own commercial and guardian responsibilities).

Governments, in turn, seeking to improve their performance capacities through the importation of ideas and people from the private sector, are similarly dependent on a strong collective culture to facilitate a sound mixture of guardian and commercial traits. Moreover, governments are increasingly engaging directly with private companies in new forms of organizational hybrid arrangements that seek a more direct fusion of resources and processes from both sectors. Corporate governance, both within each sector and for the jurisdiction as a whole, is thus an important foundation for new collaborative mechanisms that permeate many of the topics examined in this book.

Before discussing in some detail such collaborative sectoral undertakings, I examine in the next chapter how information flows across these sectoral boundaries and the use of intermediaries such as lobbyists as a means of influence. I also address how business lobbying is increasingly viewed as linked with corporate governance and stakeholder relations.

CHAPTER TWO

LOBBYING

INTRODUCTION

The previous chapter examined the emergence of corporate governance as a unique but also increasingly shared set of themes across business and government with respect to how organizations are held to account in terms of both conformance and performance. Beyond the converging challenge of establishing good governance within each sectoral realm, businesses and governments often engage in direct and indirect efforts to influence one another. Accordingly, this chapter probes the influence-laden dynamic of lobbying as the private sector, and other organized interests such as non-governmental organizations, undertake to shape the decisions and outcomes within the political and policy arenas of the public sector. I discuss the key rationales for lobbying and compare the structures and styles of lobbying in the Canadian parliamentary model and the US congressional model.

While much of traditional lobbying is predicated on managing and exploiting the separation of business and government, not unlike Jacobs' sectoral presentation and explicitly adopted as such by Stanbury, this cannot be the entire story. It is also important to consider the evolution of lobbying in a context of stakeholder governance that creates pressures for systemic learning and the co-evolutionary dynamics endorsed by Paquet. Here, then, greater demands for direct forms of engagement coupled with heightened transparency are challenging the traditional order of lobbying as influence, emphasizing instead the role of lobbying as a basis for learning.

TWO SOLITUDES

In 1987, John Sawatsky's influential book *The Insiders: Government, Business, and the Lobbyists,* exposed the growing importance of professional intermediaries in Ottawa assisting the private sector with its efforts to influence the federal government. The term "lobbyist" was rarely used initially in such circles, however, as the insiders whom Sawatsky refers to emerged during the 1970s and early 1980s as a group of consultants with political backgrounds and an eye for commercial opportunity — by providing a new type of professional service to clients.

The service was not lobbying per se (a term typically denoting an attempt to influence some aspect of public sector decision making) but government relations expertise, essentially educating business leaders about the nuts and bolts of how government works and how best to engage governments to pursue specific interests and outcomes. There was nothing unethical about this initial forte, since the professional intermediaries played a largely educational role in advising business on options and avenues for legitimately partaking in what Stanbury would term the "policy arena" in the most enlightened manner possible.

Two points are noteworthy with respect to the relationship between this initial government relations service and Jacobs' two syndromes. First, the professional consultants developing this new government relations specialization are in many ways examples of the integration or at least the bridging of commercial and guardian syndromes: leveraging political experience into a commercial pursuit. Their ability to do so supports Jacobs' notion that ultimately human beings should be able to transcend the commercial/guardian boundary, though it also suggests that the nature of these activities could prove contentious (for reasons explored below). Second, this opportunity to commercialize knowledge of guardian (i.e., government) institutions reflected a gap between the private and public sectors, an underdeveloped appreciation of one another that led to the situation where companies would seek counsel to intervene effectively.

A more recent study undertaken by the Ottawa-based Public Policy Forum (PPF) in 2002 reinforced this point, albeit with one important caveat. The report, *Bridging Two Solitudes: A Discussion Paper on Federal Industry-Government Relations*, provides a quantifiable portrait of the poor state of relations between industry and government, for each side felt misunderstood by and disillusioned with the performance of the other side:

> Government respondents see themselves as open and responsive to industry representations, and see these representations as having an impact on government decisions. They are less certain that industry understands the government's decision-making process or offers policy proposals that respond to the need of the public the government serves as well as the corporation's self-interest.
>
> Corporate respondents, on the other hand, believe they understand how government works. They believe their proposals are balanced. However, they do not believe they are adequately consulted by government. Nor do they believe their respondents have a real impact on government decisions.
>
> Such are the two solitudes.

This characterization helps to explain why those involved in the initially indirect activity of government relations (i.e., advising industry clients on how best to approach government) soon faced pressure to expand the scope of their service toward more outcome-based lobbying practices. Looking for results but frustrated with their own efforts, businesses increasingly turned to the outsiders (i.e., the "insiders," so termed by Sawatsky) to get the job done.

This trend unfolded in such a manner in Ottawa, as in most Western democracies, particularly in the Anglo-Saxon world, where the advent of free-market principles during the 1980s helped to underpin lobbying growth. This decade witnessed a dramatic expansion in professional lobbying activities at a time when pro-business, pro-market Conservative governments were in power and when few rules existed pertaining to the conduct of lobbyists and the political ideology of the governments in power was prone to resist regulating commercial activity.

The difference here lies in the fact that this particular form of commercial activity is inherently interwoven with the guardian functions of government responsible for defining and safeguarding the public interest. Such a path could only prove to be ethically contentious, particularly as governments sought to widen markets and foster greater private sector involvement in capitalist-oriented societies. While many of the ethical dilemmas had been shielded from the public purview (a key point of Sawatsky's book), some critical events involving public assets and direct contractual ties between firms and governments (and the role of intermediaries in facilitating such ties) led to growing doubts about the integrity and ethics of lobbying activities.

Planes, Trains, and Helicopters

The ill-fated attempt in the early 1990s to privatize the county's largest airport, Pearson International in Toronto, proved to be a crucial turning point for lobbying in Canada. Cancelling the deal would be Prime Minister Chrétien's first act in office following his 2003 electoral victory, the justification being inappropriate (and excessively intimate) ties between the previous Conservative government and lobbyists representing the developers, who ultimately won the long-term contract to run the airport on a for-profit basis.

Prior to 1993 and throughout much of the 1980s, lobbying activities were expanding but largely unregulated. The rationale was part novelty and part ideology — the latter typified in the United Kingdom by Margaret Thatcher's post–public office stint as a lobbyist for a large tobacco company (consistent, Thatcher argued, with the same free-market principles pursued while leading Britain's government). Indeed, as discussed below, the free-market rationale of circulating ideas and mobilizing interests around them remains a key dimension of arguments in support of lobbying activities.

Nonetheless, the same combination of novelty and ideology would also lead to a growing number of questionable interactions between the private and public sectors — and the lobbyists looking to build and exploit such bridges. The nagging but unproven allegations of inappropriate ties between former prime minister Brian Mulroney and lobbyists tied to a commercial airline purchase by Air Canada from Airbus highlight how lobbying had started to become tainted not solely and necessarily by illegal acts (objectively identifiable) but also by far more complicated and subtle patterns of ethically questionable relationships (and more subjective).

As with breakdowns in the corporate governance realm, the absence of clear rules is one dimension of this challenge. This point proved central to the aborted attempt and subsequent difficulties involving the proposed privatization of Pearson as the companies that had signed a contract to manage the airport thought that they were inappropriately penalized by the Liberal government's decision to pass legislation breaking the agreement. After several years of investigations and hundreds of millions of dollars in legal fees and settlement costs, the episode was brought to a close without any proof of misconduct by the private developers involved in the deal.

Despite this absence of guilt, most observers of the process acknowledged that lobbying activities involving various groups bidding for the highly lucrative deal had raised serious ethical questions about the acceptable boundaries of lobbying activity. Accordingly, steps were taken by the federal government to begin to introduce limited measures of transparency such as registration requirements for professional lobbyists (and those working full time on behalf of organizations), a new ethics counsellor to oversee lobbying activities and potential conflicts of interest involving private and public activities, and related efforts to encourage the lobbying industry to become more sophisticated in monitoring its own members through actions such as a professional code of conduct (created and applied to members via a new industry association).

While transparency and professionalization of the lobbying industry did occur during the 1990s, so too would breaches of trust involving questionable ties between business interests and public sector officials. The now-infamous federal sponsorship scandal and the no less salacious corruption of Toronto City Hall in a series of computer-leasing deals would, in 2005, accelerate calls for new controls and greater oversight capacities both federally and locally.[1]

The City of Toronto continued to capture headlines in 2006, with the decision of the Toronto Transit Commission (TTC) to pursue direct negotiations with Bombardier for a sole sourcing contract to supply new subway cars (232 cars at an estimated cost of $700 million). In bypassing an open tendering process, the risk was that the absence of competition could cost taxpayers. Indeed, Siemens of Germany has publicly cried foul, insisting that by building large portions of the cars overseas it could do the job for at least $100 million less. Defenders of the TTC decision (including Toronto's mayor) to go with Bombardier point out that Siemens made such claims without having seen TTC specifications and that Bombardier's pledge to build the new cars in Thunder Bay creates economic externalities for the province that should not be dismissed.

There have been no accusations of corruption (unlike the computer-leasing scandal), and what should not go unnoticed in this case is the extraordinary ability of Bombardier to lobby the public sector for its own interests while aligning these interests with those of its government clients (Schacter and Plumptre 1999). Bombardier's history is rich in this regard, having grown from strong ties with the government of Quebec while consistently cultivating positive relationships with governments first and foremost in Canada but also around the world (at times being forced to confront the favouritism of other governments). Even today, Bombardier's chief executive, Paul Tellier, is a former head of the federal public service.

At the same time, however, Bombardier is not unique: the company has long argued that most countries find ways to favour their own companies despite the rhetoric (and in some cases the formal rules of international agreements) of free trade. As the company, Toronto taxpayers, and Thunder Bay residents awaited the final outcome of what became a hotly contested political issue at Toronto City Council, much Internet blogging was devoted to arguments either favouring or opposing the sole sourcing route.[2]

It is no accident that many such scandals revolve around government procurement decisions that carry large financial implications for companies: such transactions are just one example of the unavoidable crossover at times between commercial and guardian organizations. Yet, though often less visible and reported, the influence of lobbyists on a variety of policy decisions undertaken by public sector authorities can be more pervasive and consequential.

INFORMATION INTERMEDIARIES

Despite instances of ethical lapses and dubious conduct, lobbying is both an unavoidable and a natural activity in a policy arena (as depicted by Stanbury) between two separate spheres of activity (the commercial and guardian spheres). The scarcity of information flows across both sectors—coupled with their unavoidable interactions—creates opportunities for professional intermediaries in effect to build cognitive bridges across this sectoral gulf. The alternative, an absence of separation between business and government, merely internalizes lobbying activities into more subversive interactive forms such as corruption and cronyism.

The essential role of lobbying is thus to provide information to decision makers: that such information is jaded by particular interests (e.g., clients or employers of the lobbyists) is a given and not necessarily negative. Much depends on the openness and fairness of the policy arena, an issue on which viewpoints often vary according to both political ideology and strategic interests. From the perspective of a jurisdiction's governance as a whole, lobbying can be viewed as an essential basis of information sharing much as it also plays a role in ensuring responsive government in an open and democratic society. There is, therefore, a need for balance.

The heart of the defence of lobbying as a legitimate activity is the basis of freedom of organization and expression (for its own purposes or with the aim of influencing public authorities) as principles of democratic capitalist societies. For many observers, the policy arena as depicted by Stanbury is also a marketplace of ideas where information flows are formulated and exchanged. The strength of support and the corresponding capacity to influence are thereby reflective of the merits of the ideas being put forth and the depth of support that exists either in the private sector or in civil society. For example, the declining influence of tobacco lobbyists in increasing deference to antismoking interest groups and health advocates reflects a competition in which the latter groups have now firmly gained the upper hand (at least in most Western countries).

Critics contend, however, that even if the market prism is used there are surely market failures that distort the impacts of lobbying—and thus demand public intervention to ensure the legitimacy of the process and the efficacy of outcomes. Chief among these failures are market conditions that more closely resemble oligopolies (i.e., dominance by the few and powerful) than the free-market ideal of competition with relatively few barriers to entry and organization and a corresponding multiplicity of participants.

An alternative related perspective would argue that governments are obliged to listen to and account for all stakeholders when making decisions and designing processes that ensure openness and fairness. Here the ethical prism is less about competition than about the discursive conditions for public interest–driven processes, and while such conditions may allow lobbying to occur it should not be without guidance of and rules for coordinating such activity — that is, good governance approaches suitable for processes embedded within democratic accountability systems.

Any assessment of lobbying across the OECD and North America in particular would conclude that the market prism has remained relatively intact over the past few decades (as lobbying has grown), with government regulation limiting the most egregious market failures and ethical breaches (especially those involving financial corruption). Accordingly, professional lobbying has remained largely the purview of private sector corporations and their associational bodies.

Nonetheless, the drivers for greater openness and accountability from lobbyists themselves are similar to those found within the democratic and market realms respectively. As government organizations and private sector companies face rising pressure for openness and accountability in terms of both conduct and results, the intermediaries between them are unlikely to be exempt from such pressures. As individuals and organizations, then, lobbyists can expect to face continually intensifying demands for such responsiveness, a point well illustrated by the new Conservative government's legislative centrepiece, the Federal Accountability Act, a set of measures to limit the danger that unfettered associations between private and public interests could compromise the public trust.

Although the primary focus of the act, introduced in response to the sponsorship scandal and the Gomery inquiry, is internal to the government, the overarching focus on restoring public trust also extends the scope of the legislation to interactions between government officials and those seeking to influence them. The new measures and restrictions adopted by the Conservatives may be viewed partly in response to the political perception of and opportunity associated with scandal. Yet they also reflect a broader trend in making more transparent the relationships between government officials, outside interests, and those representing them. Specific actions thus include

- a five-year ban on lobbying for ministers, ministerial staffers, and senior public servants;
- a ban on the payment and receipt of success or contingency fees;
- requirements that contacts with designated public office holders be recorded; and
- a new, independent commissioner of lobbying with a strong mandate to investigate violations under the new Lobbying Act and Lobbyists' Code of Conduct.[3]

It is noteworthy that such contemporary actions by a Conservative government are ideologically far removed from the pro-market mentality of Conservative governments in Canada and elsewhere during the 1980s. Indeed, many of the 2006 electoral promises to further regulate lobbying activities were not unlike similar calls made by the Liberals in 1993 in their Red Book platform that brought Jean Chrétien to power. A key centrepiece of the Liberal attack was the assertion that the widening scope of lobbying would lead to an Americanization of Canadian government — where financial interests and special interests seemingly hold sway over public interest determinations.

In reality, the styles and scope of lobbying vary considerably in both countries due not only to the enormous size and clout of the United States (drawing both domestic and foreign lobbyists) but also to some key structural differences between how democracy is structured in each case. Probing this comparison further helps us to understand why the main targets of lobbyists differ considerably in each country.

CONTRASTING PARLIAMENT AND CONGRESS

The aforementioned study undertaken by the PPF (*Bridging Two Solitudes*), along with its revelation of significant cross-sectoral misperceptions in terms of how business and government treat one another, nonetheless revealed a high level of consensus on who in Ottawa is lobbied and why.

This report and others demonstrate that, in a parliamentary regime, the executive branch (i.e., the prime minister, the cabinet, and the public service) is perceived as the predominant source of decision-making power, and thus it is the primary target of lobbyists. Such a perspective is in keeping with debates in Canada and elsewhere, notably the United Kingdom, pertaining to the concentration of power in parliamentary governance structures and the withering influence of the legislature in particular (Savoie 1999).

Accordingly, the PPF survey underscored the extent to which members of Parliament are perceived as having relative influence on decision making. The following ranking of targets in terms of relative importance is illustrative:

Table 1: Influence over federal government decision making

"How would you assess the current extent of the influence over federal government decision making of the following:"

	Private Sector	Public Sector
Cabinet ministers	63%	81%
PMO	60%	76%
Deputy ministers or equivalent	52%	80%
Cabinet committees	41%	50%
Assistant deputy ministers or equivalent	37%	57%
Presidents or CEOs of Crown corporations	17%	45%
Directors general or equivalent	16%	27%
Members of the House of Commons	12%	7%
Directors or equivalent	12%	11%
Parliamentary committee	12%	11%
Other levels within the public service	7%	5%
Members of the senate	7%	1%

Note: % represents percentage of those who responded either (4) or (5), with (4) being to a "moderately great extent" and (5) to a "great extent"

One important caveat to these findings is their derivation in a time of majority government in Ottawa (from 1984 to 2003, when Paul Martin would lead a minority government that would subsequently give way to Prime Minister Harper's own minority government beginning in January 2006). In a minority Parliament, it is often the case that power is more dispersed and that the legislature is emboldened to a degree surpassing that of a majority government.

Passage of the federal budget in 2005 is illustrative. Unlike Martin's tenure as finance minister (and those of many of his predecessors), when budget making was a highly centralized affair and the budget was announced in Parliament as a fait accompli, Ralph Goodale's initial version of the 2005 budget underwent significant revisions, since the Liberals required the support of the NDP to secure its passage in the House of Commons. It is possible, then, that during this time of political instability more lobbying could have been directed at Parliament and opposition leaders than would otherwise have been the case.

Nonetheless, these exceptions do not change the overall architecture of decision making and policy setting in cabinet and more specifically the central agencies (chief among them are the Prime Minister's Office and its public service coordinating body, the Privy Council Office). Notwithstanding the budget's significance, changes from parliamentary negotiations centred on a limited number of spending reallocations, leaving largely unaltered many of the specific plans of various departments and agencies under the purview of the appropriate ministers.

Where possible, lobbyists in Ottawa and provincial capitals prefer to practise a form of lobbying known as quiet diplomacy, reflecting these concentrated patterns of authority. As a result, lobbying has typically taken place in the shadows of the executive branch, outside the mainstream focus of Parliament — and by extension the media and the public. The exceptions that arise often denote the possibility of inappropriate conduct and thus scandal for the government in power.

Such a quiet and discreet approach to lobbying has proven to be particularly apt for technical issues (reflecting, it should be noted, the largest portion of government activity over its operations) that are most often off the radar screen of the average voter. On other sorts of issues, however, lobbying focuses more on the broader public to sensitize public opinion toward certain policy options and courses of action — thereby indirectly pressuring governments to act in a specific manner.

One example is the success of antismoking groups over the past decade to capitalize on research findings and solidify public opinion against public smoking, thereby creating a groundswell of support for governments to regulate social behaviour more aggressively and in many cases limit the freedoms of tobacco companies (e.g., in advertising and sponsorship) and even litigate directly against the companies.

In some instances, large companies may feel compelled to act across both levels, one such example being the financial services sector and the ongoing agenda of banking mergers. Since the government's rejection of the first proposed mergers in 1999, the banking sector has worked methodically and quietly to put in place a legislative process that at least opens the door to mergers, "subject" to a number of conditions amounting to both private and public interest tests.

Knowing full well that the latter test is interwoven with public opinion in determining the government's ultimate decision to allow or reject mergers, the banks have upgraded their public relations campaigns, research initiatives, and other such stakeholder-oriented measures designed to reassure the public about their trustworthiness. On the specific issue of mergers, banks have become much more active participants in direct political processes (e.g., parliamentary proceedings) and indirect forums such as research bodies to go beyond the technicalities of the issue and attempt to sway public opinion on the matter (especially in underscoring the modest size of Canadian banks globally and the growing frequency of mergers in other jurisdictions).[4]

Congress and K Street

With over 17,000 registered professional lobbyists operating in Washington, DC, many with offices situated a stone's throw from Capitol Hill on K Street, the patterns of lobbying and their portrayal as primarily about influence peddling remain key attributes of politics and decision making there. The coupling of federal government spending approaching a staggering $3 trillion annually and the capitalistic traits of greed and risk taking embraced as positive virtues of the entrepreneur and commercial-minded organization will invariably fuel aggressive lobbying and ethical lapses (McGrath 2005).

Few would therefore dispute the notion that Washington is the lobbying centre of the world. The reasons why go beyond the power and influence of the United States as a global superpower to include some key structural differences of power and governance in a presidential model as opposed to a Westminster-based parliamentary model.

The critical distinction is the formal legislative authority vested in Congress (formally the legislature, though described by some as the second player in a dual executive) by the Constitution that disperses power to individual lawmakers that drives lobbying strategies in the US federal capital (and similarly in US state capitals). Compare the American president's presentation of his budget, the first draft of which is usually released in January, a mere negotiating position to mark the beginnings of often tortuous negotiations with Congress; nobody mistakes the president's budgetary blueprint for the end result (unlike the customary practices of majority governments in Parliament).

On many matters of policy, moreover, domestic and foreign interests compete for influence in shaping Washington's decision-making processes in both economic and political realms. During his initial campaign for president in 1992, Bill Clinton lamented the rising authority of Japanese trade interests and the revolving door of American public servants accepting positions lobbying on their behalf; today similar concerns are often raised about China as its growing economic clout becomes evident.

Canada, too, spurred by trade disputes such as softwood lumber, has expanded its own government-to-government lobbying capacities based in Washington, attempting to go beyond the bilateral executive dimension to policy making and better sensitize individual lawmakers to Canadian interests and concerns. Without question, the ability to do so for a country of some thirty million is limited, but there is little choice for a country whose trade dependency on the American market is of paramount importance.

Aside from the division of powers, the flow of money is the other major driver of lobbying in the US system, and indeed the two are intricately intertwined. Lobbyists often aid congressional elected officials in fundraising that in turn helps to solidify their reelection prospects. Although directly bribing public officials is of course illegal, stemming the steadily rising flows of financial resources donated by special interests toward political activities has proven to be futile.

Specifically, the creation of Political Action Committees, a loophole under federal legislation that allows so-called soft money donations to underwrite the organizing efforts of politicians (mainly in preparation for current or prospective campaigns), yielded some $1.5 billion of direct financial giving from corporations and business officials during 2004 alone (Silverstein 2007). The Federal Elections Commission reported that candidates seeking election to the US Senate raised $126.6 million in the first nine months of 2005 alone. The escalating cycle of financial requirements and fundraising also reinforces the incumbency of many in Congress, making current office hours more dependent on and closely associated with donors and lobbyists.

Nevertheless, recent scandals involving the prosecution of former high-profile lobbyist Jack Abramoff illustrate the potential for such practices to corrode the public's trust of their political institutions in a manner not unlike recent scandals in Canada. Under the Abramoff affair, many in Congress were either directly bribed or indirectly tainted by ties to a now-imprisoned lobbyist who had become legendary within Washington circles for possessing great financial resources and political sway.[5]

The fallout from Abramoff and other related scandals proved to be one important theme in the 2006 congressional elections, which saw the Democrats returned to the majority party in both congressional chambers (albeit by the slimmest of margins in the Senate). As a result, in early 2007, during their first week in control of the House of Representatives, Democrats introduced new ethics legislation designed to limit the influence of lobbyists on Congress. Among many measures, the proposed bill for the first time prohibits house members and employees from accepting gifts or free travel from registered lobbyists. At the same time, discussions began with the Senate over the proposed creation of a new Office of Public Integrity to independently investigate ethics abuses involving lobbying and conflict of interest matters (not unlike the similarly empowered ethics commissioner under Conservative legislation in Canada).

While such actions are indicative of a rising tide of scrutiny and transparency over how best to ensure the integrity of the public interest, few observers would suggest that the entrenched patterns of lobbying and influence peddling are likely to change any time soon. The newly empowered Democrats, for example, stepped back from proposing a new government-run prescription drug program in January 2007, opting instead for a less ambitious plan requiring federal agencies to work with private insurers and the pharmaceutical industry to achieve lower drug prices. Along with contemplating prospects for an eventual presidential veto, Democrats were reportedly wary of the significant clout of drug industry representatives, opting instead for compromise and more incremental change.[6]

Indeed, for many in the United States, such occurrences are a welcome exhibiting of the virtuous structures of checks in a political model designed to limit the concentration of power that has come to be viewed as a key feature of the parliamentary system. In a country traditionally known for political values emphasizing personal and market freedoms, finding a workable balance between the pursuit of private interests and the assurance of public interest legitimacy is a contentious and invariably complex undertaking.

COLLABORATION AND LEARNING

In a world reflective of Jacobs' syndromes influencing one another via a Stanbury-like policy arena, we have seen that the primary defence of lobbying is that of a competitive process of ideas and access that encapsulates the principles of free markets and open democracy. Yet at the same time, if one is prepared to accept the notion that crossover and collaboration are both unavoidable and increasingly deterministic in terms of a jurisdiction's overall governance performance, an alternative prism is required as a gauge of lobbying activities.

This prism is that of social or collective learning—made possible in part by intermediaries that facilitate not only communication and exchange across sectors but also dialogue and integrative forms of action (Paquet 1997). From this vantage point, lobbyists are potentially knowledge brokers of critical importance. They can assist in the design of governance solutions that seek artful and creative compromises between different positions, at other times aligning the complementary contributions of public and private sectors in shared and integrative outcomes.

Is such a view an overly enlightened portrayal of the typical lobbyist, likely to be first and foremost an influence peddler? Generalizing across all lobbyists is not particularly helpful as a response, but what is essential to underline is how the nature of lobbying activity follows from the governance mechanisms in place that shape interactions between sectors. A competitive mindset across largely independent domains will yield lobbying that is primarily linear in seeking to maximize influence. In contrast, a more collaborative context in which sectors are viewed as largely interdependent stakeholders will encourage lobbying that is more collective in seeking to balance influence and alliance within shared boundaries.

In the recent past, this latter context was regarded and often lauded as corporatist within stakeholder jurisdictions found across much of continental Europe as well as Japan. The team-oriented spirit of such governance (although prior to the mainstream usage of this particular term) was lauded as a more strategically beneficial recipe for success in a globalizing world, creating a competition not only of companies but also of countries and societies (Thurow 1992). In contrast, Anglo-Saxon countries were depicted as overly and simplistically focused on competitive structures — as discussed here, the more natural setting for what has most commonly been termed "lobbying." Indeed, until recently in many European and Asian cultures, the term "lobbyist" has found little resonance for this reason.

As in the realm of corporate governance, there is arguably something akin to a global consensus emerging across a capitalist-laden world emphasizing a culture of governance — despite the fragility of this culture and the ongoing distinctions that remain (not unlike the relative acceptance of the shareholder/ stakeholder dichotomy across different parts of the world). This fragile global framework has resulted in lobbying as a more commonly accepted practice in Brussels, for instance, as the capital of the European Union (McGrath 2005). Furthermore, it has since become common to hear calls for closer collaboration between industry and government in the "shareholder" societies across the Anglo-Saxon world, including North America.

Yet both within and across these national and transnational governance systems, the more fundamental questions pertaining to lobbying are those of purpose and acceptance. In terms of purpose, will lobbyists continue to be viewed predominantly as influence peddlers, or are they more likely to evolve into knowledge brokers? With respect to acceptance, ultimately the citizenries of respective jurisdictions will determine the response through their indirect shaping of public institutions and the rules and cultures governing these institutions and their interrelations with private industry on the one hand and civil society on the other.

Lobbyists are not unlike private companies and public enterprises facing new pressures for better governance, particularly more open and responsive structures to respective stakeholders. As has been evident in Canada and elsewhere, the lobbying profession has itself sought greater maturity and legitimacy in recent times — facing, as has been the case for many organizations, uneasy tensions as a result. Chief among these tensions is the importance of secrecy to lobbying as a professional activity, in working behind the scenes to either influence outcomes or shape processes in some manner. If a lobbyist is identified on the front page of a newspaper, for example, it is almost without question a form of attention that is undesirable and harmful.

It is reasonable, as a result, to expect that lobbying in its traditional form of backroom influence peddling is not a sustainable prospect in a twenty-first-century governance environment featuring Internet-driven communications and openness on the one hand and more participative forms of governance on the other. Part of the debate lies with the character and conduct of lobbyists themselves (and many enlightened professionals are capable of acting in an integral manner, adapting as well to action predicated less on influencing than on learning). Yet a good portion of the shift also involves their clients — particularly companies facing increased demands for corporate governance more encompassing of wider stakeholder engagement.

Accordingly, companies face more pressure and new opportunities to bypass traditional intermediaries and undertake forms of lobbying themselves — even if such forms take on new terminology and process. Multistakeholder consultations, private-public sector partnerships, and joint ventures and alliances are the new governance venues in good currency, based in large measure on more direct forms of engagement between private, public, and non-profit actors (many examples of which pervade the topics and discussions of subsequent chapters in this book).

In today's environment, a senior manager responsible for business development in a technology solutions company, for example, is likely to be in constant interaction with public sector bodies — which may, depending on the circumstances, be clients, regulators, or partners in a variety of strategic ventures transcending direct sectoral categorization.

The resulting collaborative governance challenge, systemic in orientation, includes a language of stakeholder engagement that is common across all sectors (even as the balance of appropriate stakeholders will vary and often be contested), as is the importance of collective learning to the adaptive and performance capacities for the jurisdiction as a whole.

"Responsible Lobbying" as Stakeholder Governance

Much of the emphasis on discussions of lobbying and ethics is placed on the public sector and its ability to preserve integrity and not compromise its guardian functionality in light of either external pressures from business or other interests or internal breakdowns of controls and mechanisms for accountability. The new federal Accountability Act in Canada is a case in point, as a number of new external and internal oversight mechanisms have been introduced to ensure ethical conduct in government, much as new rules on the conduct of lobbying are primarily focused on what public servants can or cannot do.

Lobbyists also respond in kind, in some cases in direct conformance with new rules such as reporting provisions, in other cases more indirectly to respond to the new spirit of these new laws and their motivators — namely, public and by extension political suspicion surrounding their actions and conduct (and as a result their professional livelihood). Indeed, the Conservatives' efforts in this regard denote the latest evolutionary stage of a trend that transcends any particular government or country: pressures for less secrecy and more direct forms of accountability are rising, spurred by a more educated, better informed, and technologically empowered citizenry.

Although exceptions such as the security and defence realm and cabinet advice remain pronounced limitations on openness in the parliamentary system, on the whole it is becoming harder and harder for governments and lobbyists to expect anything less than demands for full disclosure of their interactions (and increasingly in real time[7]). Such a trend is similarly expanding to encompass local and provincial governments, which are following suit in designing new registries and reporting mechanisms for lobbyists.

Nonetheless, there is more to the story of the evolution of lobbying than greater demands on government (and indirectly on lobbyists) for openness. As companies themselves strive to balance shareholder returns and stakeholder relations, and as their own constituents are empowered in a manner not unlike voters, the conduct of lobbying becomes less secretive and subversive and more strategic and, as a result, subject to both internal and external scrutiny.

Stakeholder-based governance and its emphasis on productive and rewarding relational ties not only to investors and customers but also to civic and public sector bodies (which might otherwise seek to curtail corporate activity in some manner) suggest that the means of lobbying matter along with the results. They matter directly in terms of compliance with legislative and regulatory provisions (as companies not only hire external lobbyists, thereby entering into a principal-agent relationship for which they can be held responsible but also deploy their own employees in lobbying roles) and indirectly with respect to the collective legitimacy and performance of the governance system for a jurisdiction as a whole.

At this collective level, the confidence expressed in the functioning of commercial stock markets is intertwined with that of the democratic policy arena. Companies benefit when based in a well-performing governance jurisdiction: it is not by accident that the world's most transparent countries, as ranked by global watchdog Transparency International, are also the world's wealthiest.[8] The point is equally true of cities: in Toronto, for instance, local business groups have welcomed the results of the public inquiry there and efforts by the current mayor and council to strengthen governance as a basis for fair competition locally and recognition globally as a place where cronyism and corruption are not tolerated.

Accordingly, there must be expectations of sound corporate behaviour with respect to lobbying to accompany any regulation of the public sector sphere. Such expectations are an important dimension of corporate governance, and they have begun to be codified as such at the global level. Under the auspices of the UN Global Compact, and supported by several leading multinational corporations, a set of principles for "responsible lobbying" has recently been developed by AccountAbility (2005), a UK-based membership organization devoted to ethical governance in all sectors. The overriding purpose of the framework is to ensure an ethical and strategic alignment of corporate governance principles, stakeholder relations, and lobbying practices and outcomes. The report therefore puts forth a "lobbying health check" for businesses and NGOs based on the following.

- *Policy consistency:* Are we doing one thing and saying another?
- *Process transparency:* Does it look like we're trying to hide something?
- *Knowledge and people:* Does the left hand not know what the right hand is doing?

Negative answers to these questions result in a danger zone for the company, which risks negative exposure for mixed messages, poor relational ties to key stakeholders, and/or ineffective lobbying outcomes. Conversely, affirmative answers help to foster "responsible lobbying" through consistency (of the principles and actions), transparency (of associations and activities), and effectiveness (in terms of objective setting, execution, and attained results).

CONCLUSION: EXERTING INFLUENCE AND EMBRACING INTERDEPENDENCE

The broader philosophy underpinning this framework of enlightened lobbying is the pursuit of an ethical and strategic architecture for stakeholder governance based on a convergence of objectives across the traditionally separate spheres of corporate philanthropy and lobbying. Both sets of activities involve external engagements, but the former has typically been associated with an obligation for giving, whereas the latter is more strategic (and thus more in tune with actions centred on profit generation). Their interdependence lies in the growing need for a company to nurture both internal and external engagements in order to succeed in an era where cooperation and consultation are displacing or at least rivalling the traditional business emphasis on competition and communication.

Other commentators argue that with the Internet-laden information era fuelling demands for transparency, businesses have no alternative but to embrace this new mindset (Rheingold 2002; Tapscott and Ticoll 2003; Dwyer 2004). Concepts such as transparency networks and business ecosystems are now routinely deployed by industry leaders in recognition of the need to manage such interdependencies (Nelson 1998).

In such an environment, lobbying is gradually becoming viewed as less a linear process of information gathering and influencing and more a process of mutual adjustment and collaboration (Lowery 2007). As governments strive for more transparency and clarity in lobbying practices, fuelled by an ever more informed public and new forms of online media, companies face both pressure and incentives to embrace a more enlightened view of corporate action and responsibility.

One study of lobbying practices in Australia, for example, confirms this trend of immersing lobbying into a broader effort of stakeholder engagement: "In part as an extension of stakeholder engagement strategies, in part as a response to community discussion and expectations surrounding 'sustainability,' and possibly reinforced by the loss of legitimacy for business that has arisen from individual corporate malfeasance...the issues of corporate reputation and sustainability have experienced the highest increase in public affairs focus since 2000. Indeed, several major companies have replaced 'public affairs' (or its equivalent) with 'reputation' or 'sustainability' describing the overall function" (Lindsay and Allen 2005, 75).

This shift can also blur the distinction between the traditional corporate emphasis on public relations and that of public affairs. Although frequently confused, the former refers to a more generalized effort at reputation and corporate image, whereas the latter has been a synonym for lobbying. Within the realm of stakeholder-based lobbying and transparency networks, two simultaneous trends call into question the utility of maintaining this distinction: first, heightened corporate scrutiny, which is rendering PR-type activity as "spin" viewed cynically as manipulation; second, the importance of indirect lobbying efforts via media-based advertising to shape public opinion and, as a result, influence politicians (Andrews 2006).

Here the negative persona associated at times with lobbying is intertwined with broader questions of both democratic and corporate legitimacy — and the overall levels of trustworthiness accorded to both industry and government, which have been in decline in recent years (Edelman 2005). As a by-product of such concerns, leading public relations companies have themselves begun to question traditional PR "communications" in favour of more active, ongoing consultative efforts more closely aligned with the ethos of stakeholder engagement (Edelman 2005).

Yet, despite this broadening template for business responsibility and stakeholder-based lobbying, an ongoing strategic challenge for companies is to balance a competitive mindset (with its tendencies toward advertising and corporate image) with a broader set of stakeholder relationships that are becoming more prevalent in shaping key aspects of business performance. Such a tension is evident in the next challenge of the world's most successful entrepreneur-turned-philanthropist:

"Decisions about operational controls and investment are not new to Gates, Oster said, adding, 'There are also more complicated governmental issues, and certainly Microsoft has dealt with those.' But this time Gates's enemy isn't another company—it's disease, mosquitoes, ignorance, political unrest. And vanquishing those requires a different approach to partnership, she said. It will require working with a disparate group of governments, other nonprofit groups and companies that do not answer to him."[9]

Some observers would suggest that Gates' departure from his corporate duties within Microsoft (even as Gates continues to serve on the board) is indicative of the incompatibility of running a business and serving a greater good. A more cynical view is that Gates is merely countering the damage of Microsoft's antitrust difficulties with governments around the world while planting the seeds globally for an expanded marketplace for Microsoft products and services. However, it bears noting that his efforts have been under way for several years, and the new reality for businesses and their leaders is at least a microcosm of the Microsoft experience—seeking to balance effectively the short-term pressures for profitability and capital appreciation with the need to foster the collective conditions for sustaining such success (Vining, Shapiro, and Borges 2005).

Here business and government are joined by intensifying pressures for more openness and accountability within their separate realms of governance—as well as across them. The collective challenge for both sectors is to recognize lobbying as a reflection of democratic and corporate freedoms—for which the reciprocal obligation is continual accountability. Proactively seeking the conditions for ensuring this accountability is a much better bet for strengthening the performance of each sector, as well as the governance system as a whole, than what are increasingly futile efforts to shield scrutiny and manage information flows in the more routinely hidden ways of the past.

CHAPTER THREE

PROCUREMENT AND PARTNERING

INTRODUCTION

This chapter examines the expanding scope of partnerships involving the public and private sectors and the opportunities and pitfalls of explicit efforts to effectively align public and private interests. Many public sector scandals in recent years involving private sector lobbying have been driven by procurement—where the government purchases goods and services from commercial companies. Such purchasing can range from a few thousand dollars to hundreds of millions of dollars for large-scale projects, and as a result the openness and fairness of government procurement policies and mechanisms are key issues for the private sector.

Yet the traditional model of procurement, where government decides its needs and looks to the marketplace for suitable vendors, is increasingly under strain. Unlike procurement's emphasis on static contracts, where price is often the key variable, collaborative models entail what are often known as public-private partnerships. Alternative and more innovative financing schemes, risk sharing, and a basis for creativity and adaptation in a dynamic and uncertain environment are some of the main drivers of collaboration. New technologies also play an important role as government efforts to refurbish organizational capacities invariably involve the private sector, further driving the need for partnership.

TRADITIONAL PROCUREMENT UNDER STRAIN

The enlargement of business-government interactions from traditional procurement to more varied and integrative models of partnering reflects a more explicit attempt by both sectors to create successful hybrids that encapsulate elements of both the commercial and the guardian syndromes. Along with opportunities for gains to be realized by such arrangements, the dangers of doing so hark back to Jacobs' warnings if this mixing unfolds inappropriately.

In fact, it is partly the case that the traditional public sector procurement model may be viewed as an effort by government authorities to make use of both syndromes in the pursuit of the public interest. To build new roads and schools, for example, the government must engage with external contractors, more often than not specialists from the private sector. Government officials must therefore understand the basics of market activity to structure an appropriate tendering process in which companies are invited to submit proposals, which are then judged against a suitable criterion for selecting the optimal proposal.

Typically, however, the criterion used by governments is that of containing costs, an objective consistent with guardian notions of fairness and financial probity with taxpayer resources. The result is that the interactions required between government and companies are very specific—often the basis of codified agreements or contracts outlining the products and services provided and at what cost. In accordance with this cost emphasis on the one hand, and the need for governments to act fairly and openly in offering such opportunities to all prospective companies, large and small, on the other, the logic of market competition can help the government to achieve its goals. Different companies, competing with one another, face incentives to lower their prices in an effort to secure the contract.

In some respects, this approach remains in good currency today. Global trading agreements, for instance, include greater restrictions on the ability of (national) governments to discriminate between foreign and domestic firms, ideally creating more competition for business and efficiency gains for governments not only in each country but also across a globalizing world. It would be unthinkable today for any government not to engage the services of foreign and multinational companies, even as many exceptions to this trend remain in all countries (e.g., Bombardier's special status with Canadian governments or Boeing's relationship with the US military).

New technologies can only strengthen this traditional system of procurement, and governments have sought to leverage the Internet as a platform for more transparent and accessible bidding. When deliverables are fixed and easily defined, inviting submissions online is a powerful level for leveraging and aligning the incentives for commercial gain with the pursuit of public interest objectives.

Nonetheless, when deliverables are not so easily defined, and when the environment is highly uncertain, this particular form of alignment between the commercial and the guardian syndromes can have perverse consequences. The very traits of open competition meant to ensure fairness and transparency can, in turn, lead to companies submitting unrealistically lofty assessments of their abilities to contain costs and achieve the outcomes sought within the timeframes stipulated. As projects grow in complexity, and as new technologies become increasingly engrained in such projects, a vicious cycle can ensue in which the government selects a company on the basis of an unrealistic plan. As work commences, tensions invariably build between both sides, and the government faces the unenviable choices to either abandon the commercial vendor and begin the procurement process anew or salvage the existing relationship through restructured contracts that invariably escalate costs and risks.

As a result, two major sets of reasons underpin the growing prominence of public-private partnerships for the creation and maintenance of various forms of infrastructure, both new and old. They may be summarized as financing and investment on the one hand and as innovation and performance on the other. Both dimensions of seeking to combine and align public and private interests may also be interlinked within the confines of a particular governance undertaking.

PRIVATE FINANCE FOR PUBLIC PROVISION

Regarding the financing of new infrastructure, the attractiveness of leveraging private pools of capital investment is rooted in a similar context of new public management that arose during the 1980s, encouraging governments to look to industry for managerial techniques and governance practices.

A key factor in this trend had been the view that excessive government bureaucracy leads to an inefficient allocation of resources for the jurisdiction and its governance system as a whole: two alternative paths of recourse thus include either reforming government internally or privatizing specific government functions (thereby shifting them from the public to the private realm). These paths shared an emphasis on efficiency and greater sensitivity to bottom-line measures of government spending, including accumulated debt and annual deficits.

Throughout the 1980s (and in many OECD countries continuing into the 1990s), this growing fiscal sensitivity resulted in constraints on public investment perhaps more severe than at any time since well prior to the post–World War II reconstruction period, largely financed by direct government taxation and investment. The United Kingdom is illustrative, where by 1997 the British government reported the lowest levels of public infrastructure spending since the 1970s, the result being deterioration of facilities, equipment, and service standards across schools, hospitals, and other facets of traditionally public sector assets such as roadways and public transportation. In Canada, estimates of the current infrastructure gap range anywhere from $50 billion to $125 billion, with at the least a consensus that current levels of public sector spending cannot keep pace with the refurbishment needs of the country's aging infrastructure.[1]

The inability of the marketplace to respond to such a decline is indicative of what economists term a "market failure." Many such aspects of local and national infrastructure are collective in nature—used by everyone (and all or many companies) for functions of critical importance that nonetheless lack competitive structures and pricing mechanisms to warrant private investment (as there would be little hope of generating an economic return). Yet, at the same time, markets and communities suffer collectively if reparation is not forthcoming, a function invariably demanding public sector action. The question that emerges in such a context is whether or not a jurisdiction can find ways to leverage the potential benefits of private investment and competition for the pursuit of aims that are essentially collective and thus more characteristic of traditional forms of public goods warranting government investment and control.

Inspired by the warnings of Jacobs on the potentially corrupting and ill-performing hybrids of mixing the two sectors (as most traditional forms of public infrastructure are of a more guardian orientation than that of the commercial syndrome), those preferring separation and sectoral clarity would respond in the negative. Unless a particular aspect of infrastructure can be shown to be well suited to market pricing and investment (in which case the government should relinquish its involvement), the resulting public good demands clear government action and financing that is direct and unambiguous.

Conversely, defenders of integrative models of public-private activity point to the possibility of generating value from aligning complementary perspectives in a transparent manner. The *potential* benefits are well summarized in a recent report by TD Economics (2006), and they include (1) creating greater flexibility for governments in planning infrastructure development, (2) freeing up governments to focus on what they do best, (3) improving the care of public assets, (4) maintaining service quality through innovation, (5) shifting risk from taxpayers to the private sector, and (6) increasing the potential for synergies by combining project components through a single contracting party (then empowered to coordinate the project more freely than would otherwise be the case if the government managed each separate project variable).

While the concept of a public-private partnership (P3) typically denotes private sector involvement in the construction and/or maintenance of a new capital asset to be used for public interest purposes, such arrangements can take many forms. The following diagram portrays the range of such options as the product of both the risks and the levels of involvement of the private sector.[2]

Figure 1

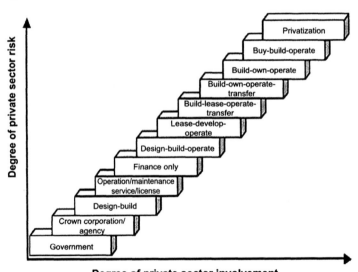

Degree of private sector risk / Degree of private sector involvement

Privatization
Buy-build-operate
Build-own-operate
Build-own-operate-transfer
Build-lease-operate-transfer
Lease-develop-operate
Design-build-operate
Finance only
Operation/maintenance service/license
Design-build
Crown corporation/agency
Government

P3s fall short of privatization—that is, the relinquishing of government involvement in favour of market ownership and private sector operations (the result of which is to negate the conditions for partnership). Most P3s typically fall in the middle ground of the above diagram, with various financing schemes involving long-term leasing arrangements and in some cases provisions about whether the asset will revert to private or public ownership at the end of the project term.

In the United Kingdom, the government introduced a scheme known as the Private Finance Initiative or PFI (Dixon, Pottinger, and Jordan 2005). Started by Conservatives but maintained and expanded under the purview of Tony Blair and his Labour government, the purpose of this program has been to create infrastructure with a public purpose through mechanisms leveraging private sector involvement in financing, construction, and maintenance. Seeking a middle ground between direct government control and outright privatization, the PFI seeks opportunities to share responsibilities and risks, creating new assets via payment schemes and commitments underwritten by the stable involvement of government authorities.

The PFI has not replaced direct public sector provision, accounting for only a modest portion of overall infrastructure spending, but it has become an increasingly prominent—and controversial—aspect of new infrastructure development across the United Kingdom. Defenders of the initiative point to the flourishing of new infrastructure projects (meeting public interest needs) that has been enabled by leveraging private sector capital investment and project management competencies while shifting much of the financial risk associated with these new ventures to industry.

Can Risk Be Shared?

Under the PFI, if a private company in the United Kingdom faces cost overruns in completing the construction of a new public facility within the agreed-to timeframe, it must absorb those costs, reducing its rate of return (thereby providing a strong incentive to remain on time and on budget). In comparison to those projects administered directly by government authorities (i.e., situating the public-private governance to the lower-left quadrant of the above diagram, perhaps contracting out limited aspects of construction to private companies but nonetheless retaining full ownership and control), studies to date suggest that

PFI initiatives enjoy stronger performance and fewer failures, and the program itself has been exported to many other countries in Europe and elsewhere (Pollitt 2000).

Yet the PFI is not without critics and controversy. The first PFI initiative led to the construction of the Skye Bridge in Scotland, connecting mainland Scotland to the island of Skye (and the stopping of local ferry services as a result). The arrangement proved controversial due to significant cost overruns by both sides: private sector operators proved incapable of sustaining profits without toll charges that rose to politically unpalatable heights. While the initiative began under the British government (then under Conservative rule), the since-created Scottish government eventually terminated the partnership and removed the tolls, reverting the bridge to a more traditional model of government control at a much greater expense than initially envisioned.

While such spectacular failures have been rare, the financial implications of the PFI remain complex and contested. From the government's perspective in particular, an advantage of the PFI or a similar public-private variant is the avoidance of up-front costs, a politically attractive prospect to any government facing short-term scrutiny over spending (usually gauged by immediate budget projections and results for which annual metrics of deficits and/or surpluses represent the most closely scrutinized performance indicator, not unlike the private sector's reliance on quarterly profits). The offsetting costs for such up-front offloading are a long-term commitment to fixed payments of one sort or another (usually specified by leasing arrangements). Some analysts contend that the cost-benefit analysis with respect to financing and return over the lifetime of the asset in question is proving to be more art than science, and a final analysis of such quantitative results may not be forthcoming for some time (Dixon, Pottinger, and Jordan 2005).

There are also ongoing questions about total costs of borrowing when investments are required for new asset construction. A key PFI rationale, as noted, has been the heightened constraints on public sector borrowing following dramatic increases in public debt that occurred in many countries throughout the 1970s and 1980s (continuing in some jurisdictions to this day). However, when left to private companies to raise capital, it may be that borrowing costs rise since individual companies are generally unable to secure the most advantageous interest rates enjoyed by government borrowers. In essence, then, governments may merely be avoiding up-front costs on their balance sheets but contributing to higher overall financing costs for the infrastructure initiative over its total lifetime (Barton 2006).

Defenders of the PFI and similar collaborative routes, however, point to the economics of risk that also play a role in shaping the most appropriate means of financing:

> The cost of public sector borrowing does not reflect the level of risk associated with an individual project but rather the ability of government to repay a loan....As a result, false economies can be incurred when a project is financed through government funding. Should the project fail, and some do, government, as the financier, will have to absorb the loss. Private sector financing brings one other benefit: another level of review and assessment. If financial institutions find a consortium's proposal to be risky, they will either refuse to finance it or charge an appropriate risk premium. This assessment then impacts on the ability of the consortium to compete with other bidders to win the P3.[3]

The sharing of risk thus involves complex models of financing and borrowing, but it also involves less quantifiable aspects such as unforeseen events that can quickly overtake many assumptions underpinning a P3 business model at the outset of the partnership. This is where a P3 becomes more than a financing vehicle—ultimately requiring a robust governance model of collaboration and flexibility to adapt to changing circumstances (Leganza 2004; ITAA 2005).

Evidence from the UK experience is unquestionably mixed in this regard, but it is important to note that PFI and other

P3 schemes continue to expand in many countries around the world, Canada being no exception. In this country, provinces such as British Columbia and Ontario are expanding their usage of P3 arrangements in core public service areas such as new health care facilities as well as extraordinary events such as the construction of new highways and facilities central to the staging of the Vancouver-Whistler 2010 Olympic Games. Indeed, across both of these realms, the BC government has established a special agency, Partnerships BC, to oversee the creation and management of large-scale partnerships, including expansion of the Sea-to-Sky Highway linking Vancouver and Whistler.[4]

Skeptics of these new governance models, both within and outside the public sector, will continue to scrutinize such arrangements, and such scrutiny is important and should be viewed as not entirely unwelcome. More than ultimately leading to a stark endorsement of public or private means in terms of new infrastructure development, the analyses and counterarguments put forth by various parties (with nonetheless varying motivations and degrees of objectivity) are indicative of the sorts of governance pressures for transparency and accountability that are becoming more commonplace across all sectors (a theme discussed in chapter 1). Along with uncertainties pertaining to cost and financing, however, are equally important questions of a more strategic nature pertaining to innovation and performance.

Innovation and Performance

As infrastructure becomes more strategic, complex, and technologically sophisticated, questions pertaining to specialized skills and capacities and the sorts of performance outcomes being sought rise in importance. For such a reason, a program such as the PFI specifically targets those areas where risk is high. If an asset is straightforward and relatively inexpensive to build, then a traditional contracting approach between public owners and private companies may well suffice; if uncertainty is high, then so is the need for leading-edge expertise and innovative solutions.

The example of highways and toll booths indicates the complexities of governance and the range of both financing and performance variables at play. In Ontario, for instance, the construction of a new toll highway in the Greater Toronto Area that began in 1993 involved an innovative partnership scheme largely because of the desire to create a more technologically sophisticated solution to driver tolls than the traditional ticketing-booth method. At the same time, the government of Ontario sought to fix its costs when tendering the project—thereby shifting risk to the private sector developers, although initial financing for the project would be arranged by a provincial crown corporation on the ground of securing lower costs of borrowing (Borins 2004). Later, in 1999, the government would sell its stake in the 407 system, moving closer to full privatization. Such a move would prove politically contentious, and while few doubt the technical success of the 407 experience debates continue about the financing and the politics of the scheme.

Indeed, the spectre of privatization would shadow the Conservative government's efforts in Ontario to embrace public-private partnering for infrastructure development, extending such efforts into the realms of education and health care. Such debate and tension would come to a head in the 2003 election campaign when a proposed PFI-type initiative for a new hospital in Ottawa drew much criticism—since the long-term lease agreement stipulated that, despite guaranteed public sector use of the facility, ownership would ultimately revert to private owners at the end of the thirty-year deal.

The Liberals criticized such an arrangement as unacceptable privatization (in the particularly sensitive health care realm), promising changes to the arrangement. Once in power, they presented a nuanced modification in the leasing agreement that would see public ownership ultimately retained in an otherwise unchanged partnership arrangement of private financing and up-front risk for a guaranteed, long-term annual payment stream. Since then, the Liberals have (not unlike the Labour Party in the

United Kingdom) sought to entrench PFI-type arrangements in a more mainstream, politically palatable template, the Infrastructure Planning, Financing, and Procurement Framework (IPFP).

The guiding principles seek to embrace private sector involvement up to the point of outright privatization of ownership:

- use of infrastructure investment as a catalyst for positive change and an enabling vehicle to achieve government policy objectives;
- long-term planning horizons;
- sound asset management, including life-cycle costing;
- modern controllership and accountability;
- value for money, including needs-based business cases to justify investment;
- collaborative investment by governments and public institutions;
- efficient financing that matches costs and benefits;
- beneficiary or user pay where feasible and in the public interest; and
- innovative engagement of the private sector to leverage expertise and capital.[5]

While Ontario has proven to be one of North America's most politically volatile jurisdictions over the past two decades (in terms of political leaders shifting dramatically across the ideological spectrum), it has also become indicative of the mainstream expansion of private sector activity across the realm of public infrastructure. New hospitals in Ontario are now being constructed under collaborative, P3-type arrangements with the private sector, and the determination of whether such deals ultimately generate net benefits for both companies and taxpayers must await a final account some twenty-five to thirty years hence.

PUBLIC SERVICE AND PRIVATE OUTSOURCING

This logic of integrative forms of public and private sector governance also extends from the creation of new, tangible infrastructure assets to the maintenance and upgrading of more digital, organizational, and often less physically tangible forms of infrastructure. British Columbia, for instance, has been Canada's most aggressive province in the utilization of "outsourcing" efforts: outsourcing involves a transfer of assets — including hardware and software components as well as people — from public sector organizations to private industry (which, in turn, provides a specialized and augmented service standard through refurbishing and better managing the asset in question).

In the marketplace, outsourcing has reshaped organizational models of companies in all industries in search of benefiting from an externalized network of partners specializing in areas outside a company's core mission. Efficiency was the key driver of outsourcing strategies, viewed as a basis for lowering operating costs via a network of externalized specialists. Yet realizing such cost savings proved elusive in many cases for a crucial reason (which continues to have relevance today for collaborative activity): namely, effectively managing these external relationships proved more difficult and challenging than envisioned.

Accordingly, there is some schizophrenia over the concept of outsourcing even among industry itself. It is viewed by some as a trend likely to continue unabated despite widening concerns about failure rates and other difficulties (Gartner Strategic Planning Series 2005b). By contrast, an April 2005 report by Deloitte Consulting paints a very different picture, calling for "a change" in the outsourcing market that will see large organizations pull away from such arrangements: "Organizations have now begun to recognize the real costs and inherent risks of outsourcing. Instead of simplifying operations, outsourcing often introduces complexity, increased cost, and friction into the value chain, requiring more senior management attention and deeper management skills than anticipated....Outsourcing is an extraordinarily complex process, and the anticipated benefits often fail to materialize" (4).

Such concerns, especially when expressed by a leading global consultant, will be used by detractors of outsourcing: a recent episode involving BC health authorities is illustrative.[6] The risks involved in undertaking external partnerships explain why some governments have explicitly chosen to forgo outsourcing in favour of different "insourcing" variants that greatly reduce reliance on the private sector as an outsourcing partner (P.A. Knowledge 2005).

Yet the countervailing danger lies in the risk of performance stagnation and the rising costs of maintaining the status quo (Reed 2004). Like all large and sophisticated organizations, governments can benefit from the collaborative logic of synergies provided the relationship dimension of partnering is taken seriously. Accordingly, the key shift from outsourcing to more enlightened forms of collaboration lies in the strategic alignment of internal and external contributions into a seamless architecture.

Information technology is a key variable. New organizational arrangements are required to underpin emerging public sector service transformation initiatives with a substantial electronic government (e-government) dimension. These arrangements are both internal to government, involving new collaborative relationships among service delivery agencies and reform of procurement processes, and external, involving the formation and management of strategic relationships between IT vendors and governments.

As more citizens flock to the Internet for online services in areas such as banking and retail shopping, governments have begun to identify parallel opportunities for the application of online services in the public sector. Initially, the impetus for utilizing online channels to deliver information and services was couched in terms of financial savings: many business models were developed by government officials and consultants demonstrating the savings accorded to online methods of service delivery versus more traditional channels such as face-to-face facilities or telephone call centres.

Most of these initial models proved to be wildly optimistic due to forecasts predicated on massive transaction cost savings from Internet communication (relative to paper and telephone) or strong, short-term growth in demand for online services, relative to other channels (Roy 2003, 2006b). Nonetheless, new organizational and technological models for delivering services both online and via more traditional channels are taking hold and beginning to generate encouraging results (Accenture 2006).

One of the most widely recognized examples of a unique service transformation involving the internal integration of government services and the establishment of a public-private partnership is that of Service New Brunswick (SNB). SNB is a Crown corporation of the provincial government that has a dual role: to provide the people and business owners of New Brunswick with the greatest ease in using and accessing government services, and to maintain authoritative public information through its three registries (real and personal property and corporate affairs).

SNB has aggressively made use of its autonomy as a Crown corporation (compared with a traditional line department) to forge collaborative relationships with industry. Central to its citizen-centric mission is the formation of "gBiz" in partnership with CGI (a Canadian technology solutions provider), a comprehensive and integrated framework for transactional service delivery. The company and the government shared in the financing of the development of this system, much as it is now sharing the revenues from licensing arrangements between CGI and other governments in Canada and elsewhere.[7] SNB now conducts more than 40 percent of its transactional business online, and it is expanding into a variety of other collaborative projects with companies designed to jointly develop solutions for New Brunswick that can be marketed and sold elsewhere (Langford and Roy 2006).

Another notable model, this time from the United States, is New York City's NYCServ Epayment Project, which is indicative of the parameters of a service-delivery architecture predicated on more citizen-centric services using a range of integrated channels (Langford and Roy 2006). "The NYCServ application streamlines and integrates three key business processes for the city of New York—processing payments, conducting adjudication hearings, and tracking towed vehicles. It has four separate revenue channels: walk-in payment centers, Internet, interactive voice response (IVR) and kiosks. The system processes 1.9 million receipts for a total of over $6 billion in 2003....It was developed by an integrated team of approximately 20 per cent Finance Department staff and 80 per cent IBM staff."[8]

Within the BC context, one example is a current collaborative undertaking between BC Hydro and Accenture Consulting that illustrates the evolution of outsourcing into new relational forms of governance tied to joint management and results-based accountability, including costs and compensations. This unique ten-year partnership arrangement is predicated on the formation of a new organizational entity, a limited liability partnership jointly accountable to both parties.

BC Hydro is contractually guaranteed to realize $250 million in cost savings over the ten-year period (by virtue of spending $1.45 billion for services that would have cost $1.74 billion under existing internal systems) as well as agreed-upon measures of performance improvement in customer service (as determined by customer service mechanisms, comparative benchmarking, and a service-level metric system formulated and utilized by both partners). To generate these sorts of results, the formation of the new entity (with limited and specified functional responsibilities[9]) enables Accenture to develop new and more innovative business processes aimed to the desired outcomes. Notably, all of the previous employees from the government agency have been offered private sector employment on equivalent salary and benefit terms, and labour representation and collective agreement terms remain unchanged.

Despite the relative novelty of this level of complexity and relational activity, the stakes in such initiatives are enormous since, if partnerships fail, so does e-government. This message was underscored some time ago: if IT projects cannot be managed well, then the infrastructure for broader organizational renewal and performance improvements can only suffer (OECD 2001). Moreover, the track record of managing IT has not been encouraging, and as discussed above there is no quick solution for how governments should organize themselves to partner, nor is there agreement on the optimal scope of partnering activity.

Yet such partnering challenges do entail dramatically different processes within government in terms of traditional purchasing (i.e., procurement) and contracting capacities. The Information Technology Association of Canada (ITAC), for example, points to the Province of British Columbia, which has been among the most aggressive subnational jurisdictions in encouraging public-private partnerships, as an example of the type of procurement to partnering reframing that is required:

> The Province of British Columbia has developed a Joint Solutions Procurement Process for the evaluation and selection of vendors in large IT projects. Its basic principle is to engage the private sector bidders in a joint discovery of the risks and benefits of the initiative to assess the capacity, commitment, and capability of the private sector bidders. The procurement process follows defined gates where information is disclosed and discussed and the field of potential vendors is finally reduced to two. The final stage engages the finalists in competing bids based on a range of criteria relevant to the business outcomes sought by the government. (ITAC 2004; Langford and Roy 2006, 8)

San Diego: From Outsourcing to Partnering

In 1999, San Diego County embarked on what was then the largest municipal IT outsourcing initiative in the world: a seven-year deal worth $644 million with a group of companies known as the Pennant Alliance (which included Computer Sciences Corporation as the prime contractor) designed to refurbish county government operations for twenty-first-century challenges.

Both sides faced real problems. A June 2002 article in a widely cited technology publication, *CIO Magazine,* declared that the deal was simply "a mess." CSC paid significant non-performance penalties that year, key executives on both sides of the arrangement were reassigned, and disgruntlement and cost overruns with an ERP initiative had the county threatening litigation.

Yet perseverance soon began to pay dividends. Constant dialogue and a real and shared commitment to flexibility and dispute settlement meant that by 2005 both sides were showcasing success. San Diego County has recently been lauded as a local e-government leader by the Center for Digital Government's high-profile municipal survey, and county CIO Michael Moore has since often reported that his IT capacities were far better off than what would have been the case had the county opted to go it alone (as some critics would have preferred) and at less cost.

Perhaps not surprisingly, then, San Diego County seemed intent on continuing down the outsourcing path. In its latest deal, the sequel, the county's board of supervisors met in January of 2007 to approve a new seven-year deal worth $667 million that extends the reliance on private sector providers for most aspects of the government's IT and telecommunications infrastructure. (The deal also carries a five-year extension option valued at roughly $500 million.)

CSC has now been replaced as the private sector partner by Northrop Grumman Corporation, selected to lead this next phase. County CIO Moore underscored that the change reflects not disgruntlement with CSC (the only other company shortlisted in the final round of the selection process) but a better proposal by Northrop Grumman. All parties expressed confidence in a smooth transition despite the inevitable complexities of disentanglement that follow seven years of CSC management giving way to a new team (Butterfield 2006).

There was also one key source of optimism that this next outsourcing phase would be successful — namely, the accumulated experiences and competencies of county management and political leaders to effectively steer a partnership of such a large magnitude. When the county first opted for outsourcing in the late 1990s, it did so in desperation. Antiquated computer systems and limited funding meant that turning to the private sector became its last and only option, hardly a recipe for a strong negotiating position. Over the past seven years, however, while leaving operations to the private consortium, the county has worked hard to expand its own strategic capacity — based within the CIO's office — to collaborate with its partner companies.

The key lesson from phase one — and a cornerstone of phase two — is that outsourcing does not mean relinquishing strategic leadership and total control to outside experts, however well qualified they may be. Instead, the basis of a solid partnership became a shared understanding on both sides of challenges, opportunities, and constraints. From this understanding flowed an accumulation of trust and relational flexibility that enabled both sides to continuously adapt to shifting circumstances as well as the unavoidable disagreements that emerge along the way.

This more balanced relationship also reassured San Diego's elected officials, who are now more inclined to follow the advice of county managers. With the novelty and constant media attention of phase one, all stakeholders were nervous and under scrutiny (a dynamic contributing to some of the early tensions that arose). A more mature political setting emerged in phase two, even as politicians kept close tabs on such an important financial commitment.

San Diego's experience demonstrates that governments need not be afraid of making long-term commitments to public-private partnerships. Sound preparation is one key, as is a governance structure that facilitates trust and shared accountability through performance metrics at regular intervals. An important lesson for industry is the public scrutiny that comes with large-scale public sector outsourcing. CSC left behind a laudable record in San Diego in this regard, as all eyes turned to Northrop Grumman's consortium and what will be achieved in the coming years.

The Government of Canada

The subnational flavour of many of the aforementioned examples (the exception being the national PFI framework of the United Kingdom) is not out of step with public sector reforms and governance innovations generally across the OECD world (Paquet and Roy 2004; Paquet 2005). Yet, clearly, with respect to infrastructure the importance of the federal government is paramount, in terms of both what it is doing and how it is doing.

Since 1993, successive Liberal governments have subscribed to the view that traditional forms of public infrastructure had been neglected. Unlike the UK model, however, the thrust of federal action has by and large been through direct government provision and intergovernmental partnering. The creation of Infrastructure Canada is a case in point: a traditional department following normal budgetary and contracting practices of the federal government, the entity has sought to direct federal funds to local communities via competitive selection and contracting mechanisms.

While limited examples of a private-public variant, alternative service delivery, have been deployed, the federal government has generally been viewed as cautious in its handling of infrastructure development of traditional bricks-and-mortar forms, in large part due to the political visibility accorded to the spending initiatives in communities across the country. The relatively lower risk levels associated with many such projects (focused on facilities such as roads, community centres, and the like), coupled with the availability of public funds (facilitated by accumulated and growing federal surpluses), arguably diminished the pressure for innovative financing models such as the PFI and other P3 variants that have become more common elsewhere.

The federal government has shown a similar distrust of increased private sector involvement, even in the realm of e-government and its own organizational infrastructure, where weak partnering capacities between the sectors are increasingly viewed as a vice on the digital refurbishment of the government of Canada (Langford and Roy 2006; Roy 2006b). This is not to say that the private sector is not actively involved in supplying the federal government with its technology needs; rather, traditional contracting and procurement mechanisms have largely been retained. Much of the online service delivery architecture for the flagship Government Online program, in particular the secure channel (i.e., the secure network facilitating online exchange), was built through private sector expertise, albeit via tightly administered contracting to internalize much of this new apparatus (as opposed to the outsourcing variants of British Columbia, San Diego, the United Kingdom, and elsewhere).

Despite this caution, and in much the same manner that the PFI has both critics and defenders, it is difficult to conclude outright that the federal government has suffered from its choices — lauded as the world leader in e-government transformation by one leading organization from the private sector itself. Indeed, international studies suggest that no approach is without risk and that no approach has been a proven success (Dunleavy et al. 2003).

There is nonetheless widening consensus in Canada that (1) the private sector role is underutilized and frustrated by traditional procurement practices (often paralyzed by the reverberations of scandals in recent years such as the sponsorship inquiry and the much-bungled gun registry project) and that (2) more governance experimentation involving private-public collaboration will be required in the future, a point acknowledged even by federal government authorities (PWGSC 2005).

The arrival of a Conservative government in 2006 may provide a turning point in this regard, although one important lesson to draw from the preceding analysis is the increasingly strategic nature of collaborative governance choices as a widening spectrum for new infrastructure development less rooted in political ideology than a practical balancing of financing and innovation in a manner that best integrates public interest needs and private sector competencies.

CONCLUSION: COLLABORATIVE LEGITIMACY

An important current running through the themes and examples presented in this chapter is the widening acceptance of mixed forms of public and private organization. Although not without controversy and scrutiny, a mix of pragmatism, humility, and creativity underscores the growing needs of government to work effectively with business.

Nonetheless, for such pragmatism to be workable, it must pass the test of public legitimacy that comes with any governance or policy-making process under the rubric of democratic accountability. Here lies the added dimension of relational complexity for governance arrangements transcending sectoral boundaries: first, structuring an appropriate balance between the private gains (i.e., profitability) that sustain market action and the public interest scrutiny and accountability inherent in democratic states; second, allowing the governance mechanisms for such collaborative ventures to evolve and adapt in light of changing circumstances, balancing public sector oversight and controls with shared capacities for mutual learning and adjustment.

With respect to outsourcing arrangements, for example, such interfirm agreements generally remain the exclusive domain of those companies involved (with some limited oversight by shareholders via boards). In other words, in the absence of unusual, illegal, or unethical behaviour, corporations enjoy greater degrees of freedom to achieve shared performance outcomes over time than will be the case for a public-private partnership.

Any tendency by governments and their private partners to shield such scrutiny, however, often through secrecy provisions in contracting and layers of technical complexities, is likely to be misguided and counterproductive. The view that secrecy breeds suspicion is increasingly true in all governance settings — particularly when governments and democratic accountability are involved (Barton 2006).

The essentials of transparency and fairness thus create a strategic conundrum for governments in terms of processes for selecting partners (for either the outsourcing of internal assets or the creation of new infrastructure externally). Whereas legitimacy in intermarket relations is derived primarily (though not exclusively) from within corporate structures, vested in the ranks of senior managers, the legitimacy of government's selection involves process considerations that must be above reproach not only politically but also across all private sector participants vying for the upper hand.

An important challenge for government is therefore to orchestrate the conditions for public-private interactions. Such conditions require moving beyond the linear influencing patterns of Stanbury's policy arena and fashioning a dialogue that can serve as a basis of learning (Yankelovich 1999). Learning serves to transform the adversarial conduct of lobbying into a process of mutual accommodation, compromise, and (to the degree possible) agreement on at least some basic principles for guiding decisions.

In the realm of telecommunications and digital infrastructure, the increasingly networked nature of security challenges, for instance, means that this capacity for collective learning is increasingly central to both stability and adaptability for a governance jurisdiction as a whole. Questions about security and privacy are thus front and centre in the digital nexus between industry and government, which is an increasingly prominent dimension of relational governance between the two sectors, and this is the focus of the next chapter.

CHAPTER FOUR

SECURITY AND PRIVACY

INTRODUCTION

Since September 11, 2001, many national governments have been emboldened to undertake aggressive, preventive strategies aimed at public safety and the circumventing of terrorism. As a result, new technologies viewed during the 1990s as primarily a platform for electronic commerce are now front and centre in underpinning government efforts to gather, process, and share information to maximize the prospects for collective security. This expanded security imperative carries important consequences for individual identities and personal privacy: one prominent CEO has even questioned the feasibility of safeguarding privacy in an increasingly virtual and interconnected world. Others worry that aggressive security action by government authorities may unnecessarily trump personal and market freedoms, cornerstones of democracy and capitalism, while fostering enlarged and secretive bureaucracies insufficiently accountable for their actions.

The virtualization of security and the implications for privacy also carry enormous consequences for business. First, digital security is increasingly a networked challenge as online connectivity and interoperable computer systems enjoin all sectors (and increasingly all countries) in a manner that defies centralized safeguards and controls. Second, private companies often possess the very information on consumers that governments believe they need to target threatening activity: new sectoral tensions are thus apparent in terms of the legal and less formal obligations of companies to collaborate with government on the one hand while appropriately accounting for the rights and interests of their customers on the other. For other companies, however, this expanded security creates new opportunities to sell technological systems and services to public sector bodies — further intensifying lobbying efforts as well as the sort of collaborative activity examined in the preceding chapter. With both commercial opportunities and security threats transnational in scope, countries must navigate these relational governance challenges not only domestically but also beyond traditional notions of national borders.

NETWORKED SECURITY

Today's global telecommunications infrastructure has undeniably proven resilient in underpinning a global economy now estimated to be surpassing some US $60 trillion in total production. In terms of online commerce specifically, Forrester Research predicted nearly $7 trillion in transactions in 2004 (inclusive of both business-to-business and business-to-consumer transactions). Visa International alone reported more than $150 billion in 2004 e-commerce activity, with online sales representing 7.4 percent of all transactions (16 percent of all transactions crossing at least one national border).

Unfortunately, despite such an expansion of legitimate online commerce, there can be no claims of digital nirvana, since the Internet has been equally adept as a platform for organized crime, terrorism, and child exploitation.[1] More subversive threats also persist, as criminals deploy an expanding array of techniques to steal identities and victimize both individuals and organizations. Accenture consulting, for example, reported that the total costs from identity theft were expected to approach some $2 trillion globally in 2005. The CSI/FBI computer crime and security survey of the same year reports a reversal of what had been a modest decline in unauthorized system breaches in recent years.[2] Not a week goes by without media stories of information mishaps, and there is a growing view, even among the most conservative experts, that cybersecurity — or the lack of it — denotes a highly exposed underbelly of the new economy (Scalet 2006).

As a result, the explosive growth of the Internet's first decade has moderated, and security and privacy concerns are important factors in the trepidation of many to move online (Bryant and Colledge 2002; Hart-Teeter 2003). A 2005 Ipsos Group survey in the United States reported that the percentage of Americans banking online stalled at 39 percent, with nearly three-quarters of those shunning online channels invoking concerns about personal privacy and the secure storage and processing of their financial information (Roy 2006b). Paradoxically, many surveys in the United States and Canada demonstrate that banking institutions are by far the most trusted organizations for processing personal information online.[3] In Statistics Canada's 2005 Internet Use Survey, 75 percent of respondents expressed concern about privacy and security online (Roy 2006b).

A major challenge in discerning the meaning and motivation of such "concerns" is the lack of consensus inherent in any democratic-minded, capitalist society about what constitutes an appropriate level of privacy. From a service perspective, new trade-offs between privacy and convenience are unavoidable, much as they are between privacy and surveillance in light of threats to public safety and security.

If a useful definition (albeit one of many) of privacy is "the condition of being left alone, out of public view and in control of information that is known about you,"[4] the major threat to privacy in an increasingly digital society is the difficulty of upholding such information control while participating in transactional and associational activities across commercial, societal, and political realms. Individual viewpoints will vary as to what, if anything, should be done. One widely cited approach, for instance, segments the public three ways: the privacy fundamentalists (highly concerned and engaged), the pragmatists (prepared to trade some privacy), and the unconcerned (who think little of the issue).

Such trends reveal the dilemma facing both industry and government in promoting online service channels as a means to improve efficiency and performance. Furthermore, as discussed in the previous chapter, the pervasive nature of digital infrastructure means that both sectors are also interlinked in their reliance on widely distributed technological systems. Safeguarding privacy is therefore a pervasive issue that cannot easily be ascribed to any one organization.

A report prepared for the European Union in 2002 invokes the concept of "network security" as an overriding challenge in ensuring prosperity and stability in an increasingly interconnected and informational environment: "Network and information security can...be understood as the ability of a network or an information system to resist, at a given level of confidence, accidental events or malicious actions that compromise the availability, authenticity, integrity, and confidentiality of stored or transmitted data and the related services offered by or accessible via these networks and systems" (European Commission 2001, 11).

The heightened risks from an absence of networked security have become steadily more apparent to both governments and business leaders since. A 2006 report by the US-based Business Roundtable, a CEO council of many of America's largest companies,[5] points to the absence of sufficient collaboration between sectors as a critical weakness in the underlying technical and governance architecture of a socioeconomy ever more reliant on digital underpinnings: "Progress has been made over the past 10 years on technical issues...but strategic management and governance issues have yet to be addressed....Should a cyber-attack or massive Internet failure occur, well-intentioned government officials and industry leaders are not currently in a position to synchronize efforts to deploy coordinated and tested capabilities to restore Internet services. In addition, the nation's political and business leaders are not prepared to manage public trust issues, such as confidence in the markets, in the event that cyber-restoration efforts are unsuccessful or appear uncoordinated" (Business Roundtable 2006, 1).

The warnings by the US Business Council are accompanied by mounting public concerns in the overall resilience of today's pervasive digital infrastructure. For instance, an annual survey of the American public by the Cyber Security Industry Alliance consistently yields high levels of networked insecurity:

The group claims categorically that, "by any measure,

Table 2: Digital Confidence

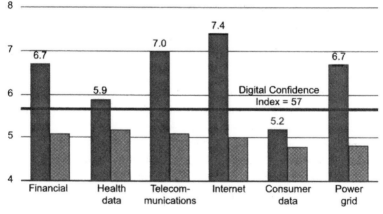

Americans are not experiencing a gain in confidence when it comes to computers and other machines that bind them."[6] Such concerns, in the country hosting the largest proportion of the world's Internet users, may cast doubt on the sustained expansion of online activity. Yet they do not appear to be stunting the determination of governments and businesses to introduce new technologies under the purview of antiterrorism.

BIOMETRIC IDENTIFICATION AND RFID

These various currents underscore the necessity of interoperability and interdependence on the one hand and the present realities of governing in a more independent manner on the other. Since the former set of pressures can be expected to continually intensify, in a manner intertwined with economic integration, how the Canadian polity responds is an important question for both individual citizens and businesses. An equally important question, however, is whether the Canadian response is merely a reaction to US pressure or a genuine attempt to rethink both domestic and continental mechanisms for reconciling identity and interoperability issues into the foreseeable future.

Concerns about the Patriot Act have done little as yet to quell cross-border traffic and the desire of companies and citizens from Canada to seek US access, but pressures are intensifying for more integrative action across the two countries. The first barrier erected in the post-9/11 environment to this relative free flow of individuals (at least pertaining to leisure travel, as professional and employment restrictions are more varied and common) focused on Canadian landed immigrants. Beginning in March 2003, landed immigrants in Canada from many countries faced new visa restrictions. Subsequently, in April 2005, the US government announced that, by the end of 2007, Canadians entering the United States will require a passport or a like-minded form of "secure identifier." Although the transition period is regarded as a cushion to soften the blow of this important change (in 2002, roughly one-quarter of all Canadians held a valid passport), its significance is profound.

Ironically, this policy change was announced just a few weeks after the release of a trilateral North American study (under the auspices of the US-based Council on Foreign Relations) that argues for the formation of a continental security perimeter as well as a set of institutions to forge the sort of North American "community" that might one day lead to less restricted mobility within the continental perimeter along with some form of standardized identification to facilitate such openness while preserving security.

These questions converge around the sensitive issue of whether Canada will introduce a new identification card, either through or parallel to beefed-up passports that make use of biometric devices and new technological standards (Roy 2006c). By the end of 2005, at least four European countries (Belgium, Germany, Sweden, and Norway) had begun implementing biometrically enabled passports, with many other countries, including the United Kingdom, having already tabled their intentions to follow suit.

The EU framework for passports and travel documents has been an important enabler, as have standards endorsed by the International Civil Aviation Organization (ICAO). Although pressure to adapt to new US entry requirements is clearly one factor motivating these actions of European countries (notwithstanding the fact that the US federal government has not kept pace with its own technological upgrading of passports), another factor is a broader digital governance strategy at both domestic and European levels that includes both service and security aims.

Biometric tools that embed a unique physical or genetic trait (e.g., a fingerprint or retina scan) are increasingly viewed as inevitable in this regard, not only for service integrity and better delivery but also for national security. Indeed, already biometrics are becoming common in a range of uses, including passports and smart cards, immigration assessment systems, Disney parks, and beachfront bars, which view them as a promising alternative to carrying cash (Roy 2006c).

Nonetheless, biometric devices remain infantile in usage, and the potential for an erosion of privacy is of particular concern. Had it not been for 9/11, such questions would surely mean insurmountable barriers for any North American government in which pre-2001 suspicion about expanded information holdings ran high (recall the federal government's HRDC firestorm in the late 1990s surrounding plans to create an integrated national database of personal information, once again envisioned as a means to better coordinate and deliver services).

From the private sector vantage point, this digitization of governance is a complex set of opportunities and constraints shaping industry-government interactions. Some companies and industries may incline to resist new identity and security schemes as inconsistent with the principles of freer trade and more open markets. For other companies, however, especially those in the technology sector, these developments create plentiful opportunities to offer products and solutions.

As with most other forms of infrastructure discussed in the preceding chapter, government choices about whether to insource or outsource new mechanisms matter greatly to industry. Across Scandinavia, for example, a single company (Setec, since acquired by Gemplus) has been the leading private sector contractor in developing new passport systems, whereas Germany has opted for a more limited use of private sector involvement, purchasing microchips and other elements of a solution integrated and produced by the German Federal Printing Office.

In this manner, many of the recent, post-9/11 efforts across the Anglo-Saxon world have begun to converge closer to the traditional European model of closer public-private collaboration. There is evidence that increasingly countries view these security-laden initiatives as an important means of endogenously promoting technological expertise and commercial applications within their jurisdictions (Strickland and Hunt 2005). The more rapid adoption by Benelux and Northern European nations of biometric devices reflects not only the well-advanced stages of technological deployment across both government and industry (as well as the traditionally strategic and closely aligned efforts of both sectors) but also greater levels of public support for government-sponsored interoperability strategies, which have become the hallmarks of digital connectivity and service integration (Lau 2005).

Still, these measures have not been without criticisms, especially pertaining to the technological choices and systemic resilience of new schemes. In Norway, for example, "the Norwegian Data Inspectorate expressed serious concerns regarding the security of the new passports, and in particular the fact that the data stored on the RFID chips is not encrypted. This represents a potential threat to personal privacy and could lead to forgery and identity theft, the Inspectorate said, adding that uncertainties also remain concerning the storage of biometric information in a central database and the use of such a database."[7]

RFID, or radio frequency identification, is a good example of how new digital technologies shape the separate actions of businesses and governments as well as their interrelations. Since RFID tags can be applied to most anything, including products and people, the consequences are significant. Supply chain mechanisms, inventory management systems, and the governance of shipping and transportation generally all stand to change considerably, often with noticeable service improvements for the user. For example, in 2006 New York City conducted a pilot RFID project enabling travellers to enjoy automatic entry and payment via a smart card.

Yet the same technologies can also allow governments to impose rigorous new rules on private sector companies in the name of better security. A March 1, 2006, cover story of the prominent technology-centric publication *CIO Magazine* entitled "Customs Rattles the Supply Chain" revealed the depth of the plans of the US Department of Homeland Security for improving the security of maritime ports and distribution systems, which manage more than 9 million incoming containers each year.

Central to the federal government's post-9/11 effort (which attracted renewed attention in 2006 in the aftermath of the scuttled takeover of several US port facilities by a Dubai-based company) is a voluntary registration program for companies to vouch for the security of their global supply chains. As a result, many companies such as General Electric have begun deploying RFID technologies to better track their shipments and their handling, while port authorities in Hong Kong, the Netherlands, and elsewhere have started to deploy high-tech scanning devices to inspect incoming goods.

A significant concern for US industry is that such voluntary measures are expected to become formal requirements in the next several years. There is little agreement about whether the financing mechanisms for incurring the billions of dollars of new costs are best viewed as private, commercial interests, thereby left to companies to incur and pass along to consumers as need be, or a form of public interest better funded from general government revenues or new taxation measures specifically levied on the shipment of goods (Haveman and Shatz 2006).

The choices made by the federal government will partly be determined by the lobbying dynamics of Stanbury's policy arena. Large American retailers such as Wal-Mart have been accused by some stakeholders of aggressively lobbying the federal government to refrain from tighter security restrictions (AFL-CIO 2006). The issue is a good example of how different industries often have diverging viewpoints on the appropriate course of action: while some companies fear disruption of their global supply chains, others see opportunities for new technological deployments and service contracts to make such deployments workable.

The lobbying and policy dynamics of the United States, in turn, shape the Canadian scene. Port authorities in this country have been quick to underscore the risk of underinvestment (and by extension the need for more public investment) in Canadian port facilities that could attract the ire of US authorities — in addition to heightening the risk of terrorist attack in this country (distribution flows shared between the two countries from third parties are a significant source of overall traffic, and major Canadian ports lie close to the United States) (Ircha 2003).

Port authorities thus walk a fine line — seeking maximum financing from the public sector on the one hand and limited regulatory obligations on their operations on the other. Their ultimate success is the result of a complex equation involving not only the effectiveness of direct and indirect lobbying strategies but also the shifting public mood (and resulting political pressure) in response to critical events that either heighten or diminish the prioritization of Canadian port security.

While there is much speculation about prospective uses of RFID in security and public safety mechanisms involving people (e.g., tracking provisions for persons of interest), more widespread use in commercial realms such as retail is quickly becoming a reality. Ontario's privacy commissioner, Ann Cavoukian, underlines that, in understanding the impacts of RFID on individuals and society, it is not the technologies per se that matter but the broader information and governance systems within which they are embedded. She further argues that "RFID information systems should be as open and transparent as possible, and afford individuals with as much opportunity as possible to participate and make informed decisions" (Cavoukian 2006, 2).

As with new electronic passports and port security, technology is a key dimension of RFID, but as Cavoukian points out, technical use matters less than societal adoption and the ability of all sectors to work openly toward a responsive governance covenant. The resulting consequences for individual, organizational, and collective accountability are increasingly pronounced, as illustrated by one Canadian citizen, Maher Arar.

M. ARAR AND JOSEPH K.

Despite the tendency to equate concerns about identity and privacy with the post-9/11 focus on terror, the roots of such debates are much deeper, intertwined with the rise of the "computer state" and both its positive and its negative potentials (Burnham 1980). Most recent variants of concern tied to the emergence of e-government stem from the 1990s and the efforts of government to utilize new technologies to reduce waste and fraud on the one hand and to better service integration and delivery on the other. Both themes remain prevalent in many jurisdictions, notably the

United Kingdom, where the British government has attempted to downplay the antiterrorism dimension in response to critics of a new national ID card now being implemented.

There can be little question, however, that 9/11 marks a critical turning point in the public sector's use of new digital technologies—underpinned by a public more readily prepared to sacrifice privacy for security (Hart-Teeter 2004). Despite higher support for security aims in most countries, how government and industry gather and utilize information has become an increasingly contentious political area in both the United States and Canada (with many issues enjoining both countries in some manner).

The Syrian-born Canadian citizen Maher Arar came to Canada in 1987, subsequently earning a master's degree and finding employment as a telecommunications engineer for an Ottawa-based company. In September 2002, returning from a trip to Tunisia on a stopover in New York, he was detained by US security officials, questioned, and eventually deported from the United States to Jordan and then to Syria, where he would be interrogated, imprisoned, and tortured for more than a year. Upon his return to Canada in late 2003, his crusade to shed light on what he alleged to be a groundless campaign against him resulted in the formation by the Canadian government of an independent public inquiry (or Commission of Inquiry) to examine this affair.

The inquiry, led by Justice Denis O'Connor, reviewed the actions of Arar and all Canadian officials as well as all pertinent information gathered by the government. The inquiry's first report, completely exonerating Arar of any terrorist action or affiliation, provided a considerable indictment of actions undertaken by the Royal Canadian Mounted Police, ultimately leading to the resignation of its commissioner. O'Connor then examined the need for new oversight mechanisms for the security-related actions of the RCMP and other federal agencies engaged in security efforts. These recommendations put forth in the commission's final report, tabled in late 2006, are to be acted upon in some manner by the Conservative government in 2007.

Despite Arar's exoneration and $10.5 million in financial compensation from the Canadian government), the case raised many concerns about systemic secrecy and performance. Even after the inquiry's final reports, for instance, legal battles are ongoing over the refusal of the government to publicly disclose large amounts of information gathered during the proceedings.[8] For many, Arar's misfortune exposed the dangers of an overly aggressive security state that would otherwise be beyond scrutiny.

How governments and corporations make use of widening interoperability in their pursuit of both commercial and public security objectives involves what some see as an increasingly ubiquitous and invisible infrastructure extending across the realms of both government and commercial activities: "Law enforcement and intelligence services don't need to design their own surveillance systems from scratch. They only have to reach out to the companies that already track us so well, while promising better service, security, efficiency, and perhaps most of all, convenience. It takes less and less effort each year to know what each of us is about....More than ever before, the details of our lives are no longer our own. They belong to the companies that collect them and the government agencies that demand them in the name of keeping us safe" (O'Harrow 2004, 300).

The governance dilemmas that result have been well summarized by Solove (2004) through two contrasting images — one familiar, the other somewhat more novel. The first image invoked, and ultimately rejected by the author, is the Orwellian notion of "big brother" that often accompanies critics of government schemes aimed at greater information gathering and public surveillance. Such steps are viewed as a loss of civil liberties and personal freedoms that, if taken to an extreme, can result in the sort of omnipresent, control-minded state apparatus that characterized George Orwell's dark vision of the world in 1984 (as Orwell portrayed it upon the book's release in 1949).

Such a vision is surely not without at least some resonance in today's world. The increasing usage of video surveillance and wiretapping capacities, and the expansive virtual systems of identity authentication, credit authorization, and service transactions that now pervade our society all fuel the view that privacy is a figment of the past for those living in the developed, digital world. "Privacy is dead," famously quipped Scott McNealy, former CEO of SUN Microsystems, urging consumers to accept it and "get over it."

Those suspicious of an emerging Orwellian state might look to the Netherlands, where the government will, beginning in 2007, assign to each new baby an electronic file that is meant to record personal and domestic information on the person as he or she matures, thereby enabling public authorities to better plan for and deliver public services. Steeves and Kerr (2005, 1) argue that cyberspace is becoming a "data-minefield" for children due to "commercial imperatives that seek to embed surveillance deeper and deeper into children's playgrounds and social interactions." Efforts by governments in non-democratic countries, notably China, provide further ammunition, as even the American Internet giant Google, which legally fights its own government at home to preserve proprietary information, succumbs to pressures by Chinese authorities to effectively censor Internet searching in the largest developing country in the world.

Yet where this image breaks down is in the tremendous technological and organizational leap of control and containment capacities that would be required to approach anything resembling an Orwellian society. As far reaching is the total breakdown of political oversight and civic resistance that would be necessary to allow for such dramatic government intrusions into all aspects of social and economic life. In contrast, some early observers of the digital politics era noted that technology may also give rise to counterclaims — of governments today confronting a sort of reverse Orwellian syndrome where their actions and decisions are increasingly probed and scrutinized at a relentlessly increasing pace (Alexander and Pal 1998).

The culture of secrecy is thus not sustainable, and it is unthinkable in a reasonably democratic and open society to envision government's achieving — or even attempting to achieve—anything resembling Orwellian control. Recall once again that the technological prowess of Scandinavian countries that fosters widening information interoperability across private and public authorities alike is accompanied by unparalleled levels of democratic transparency and managerial openness within the public sector.

For such reasons, Solove (2004) prefers the invocation of Franz Kafka's infamous portrayal of *The Trial* that ensnares the hapless Josef K. in a web of bureaucratic mystery and legal secrecy that would claim first his freedom and ultimately his life. In Kafka's disturbing world, the defendant, Josef K., is summoned to an otherwise unacknowledged court whose proceedings seem at once random and improvised. The charges against him are never revealed, and as the defendant searches for process and order he finds only a stubbornly unresponsive bureaucracy accountable only to itself. Although he is not remanded in a physical sense, Josef K.'s involvement in the trial invariably pervades his relations with friends and family, colleagues and neighbours, and above all himself (his faculties are thus worn to the point where his ultimate execution seems to come as almost pathetic relief in ending the ordeal).

In June 2006, three detainees at the infamous American prison camp in Guantanamo Bay committed suicide; despite reportedly numerous attempts by inmates, these cases were the first reported self-inflicted deaths. In May 2006, a report by the Council of Europe found that many European countries secretly colluded (by either tacit approval or feigned ignorance) with the American CIA in transporting uncharged terrorist suspects to a network of secret prison camps (the locations of which remain a source of contention within the European Union). It was, in fact, under the auspices of an EU investigation into this affair earlier in 2006 that led Maher Arar to travel outside Canada for the first time since his return from detention in Syria in order to testify in front of European parliamentarians.

At the heart of the relevance of Kafka's trial as dangerously analogous in some manner to today's War on Terror, and the methods of democratic governments to maintain public safety, is the danger of expanded state action (often through bureaucratic enlargement and heightened secrecy) in a manner unaccompanied by openness and accountability. While terrorism has yet to bring down democracy, in this respect Michael Ignatieff (2004, 80) argues that its impacts can be more subtle in nonetheless weakening it from within: "When terrorists strike against constitutional democracies one of their intentions is to persuade electorates and elites that the strengths of these societies — public debate, mutual trust, open borders, and constitutional restraints on executive powers — are weaknesses."

Maintenance of a proper balance between covert and effective action and democratic and legal checks and balances is therefore not easy. Defenders of current government action, moreover, point to rising terrorist threats — and examples of abuses and potential abuses (e.g., those noted above) — being publicly debated with alterations in actions and policies resulting. In Canada, along with the anticipated release of findings from the Arar inquiry itself, the Supreme Court began hearings on the first ever challenge to Canadian antiterrorism legislation in June 2006, just days after an RCMP-led effort to dismantle a suspected terrorist cell based in the Greater Toronto Area that had been plotting to gather explosive materials and target Canadian political and policing institutions.

Critics have contended that legal proceedings against the suspects have been shrouded in secrecy, with much information held by the Crown protected by national security laws. Yet, at the same time, the intense media coverage itself is an important source of scrutiny (if not accountability), and Canadian law enforcement officials took the unusual but seemingly constructive step of reaching out to the Muslim community by way of outreach sessions and regular briefings. The absence of civil unrest or widespread public outcry about the handling of the cases, at least early on, suggests systemic stability and public support for the police action and judicial proceedings.

To keep pace with terrorist and other forms of criminal activity that are proliferating online, law enforcement authorities are turning increasingly to more aggressive forms of virtual monitoring, analysis, and surveillance. While the Patriot Act has received much attention both inside and outside the United States, it is but one element of a broader set of informational measures that have grown rapidly since 2001. With respect to data-mining—the creation of computer programs to troll billions of electronic records in search of identifiable patterns of behaviour—the US federal government has greatly expanded its use of such techniques (at times making use of the record holdings and gathering competencies of companies such as Choice Point), though the precise parameters of spending and intent are elusive due to disclosure restrictions.

Even though data-mining has proven effective as a research technique in settings where the information base is limited and controllable, deploying such techniques on the scale of what is being pursued by national governments is a much more contentious and less certain proposition. In one notable experiment, the US Department of Homeland Security is said to have spent more than $200 million following 9/11 on a project known as CAPPS II, attempting to comb airline passenger records and assign levels of risk to each passenger boarding a plane. The project has since been abandoned since it never proved effective in correlating information sources such as credit worthiness and prospective terrorists (Mohammed and Kehaulani 2006).[9]

This false start notwithstanding, the US government has since expanded its efforts in the realm of airline passenger information, demanding the detailed flying records of not only domestic airlines but also any transportation company flying over (and not necessarily landing in) American airspace. The Canadian federal government has been developing similar programs involving Canadian airlines, and indeed in most areas of antiterrorism activity actions by the US government inform those of Canadian authorities.

NEW SECTORAL TENSIONS: LOBBYING AND LEARNING

The post-9/11 fixation on security that has recast the priorities and organization of many governments, particularly those at the national level, is a case in point. A closely related aspect of this focus is the increasingly virtual dimensions of information flows and governance systems that may elude conventional forms of assigning responsibility and accountability. The more complex and secretive a government system, the greater the likelihood for traditional forms of lobbying that are otherwise being challenged as ethically corrosive and a threat to the trust and legitimacy of democratic institutions.

It is not surprising that the focal point of such concerns is Washington, DC, where the post-9/11 formation of the colossal Department of Homeland Security (DHS) has been characterized by some observers as a "huge honey pot" for professional lobbyists, many of whom have become lobbyists in this field by virtue of past government experience.[10] As in Canada, some restrictions are in place to limit such crossover, but their overall impact does little to blunt the nexus between lobbying and homeland security activity. One of the most sought after lobbyists in Washington of late has been former Attorney General John Ashcroft, who, while being restricted in his ability to lobby the Department of Justice, formerly under his domain, faces no such restrictions in lobbying DHS, a body with which he dealt constantly while serving in cabinet (see Wayne 2006).

The ethically potent mix of urgent public interest action and mobilizing private interests would become the focus of an online story by a widely read Internet blog, Motherjones, in 2002. Something of a derivative of both Sawatsky's label, The Insiders, and Jacobs' commercial and guardian syndromes, the article's title, "Security Traders," encapsulates the intermixing of private gain, government action, and lobbying:

> Following September 11, the private sector was quick to offer its assistance, and its products, to the federal government.

The Federal Aviation Administration was besieged with 23,000 proposals for new airline security devices, ranging from "smart" closed-circuit television systems to minivan-size explosives-detection tools. "We've got every salesman — 20,000 of them, I think — approaching us about how they've got some machine that will take care of everything," Transportation Secretary Norman Mineta told the Senate Appropriations Committee in May.

Congress has criticized the specifics of Bush's plan, but few on Capitol Hill have seemed inclined to challenge the president's proposed level of homeland-security spending. And companies are getting the message. "It's free government money right now," says John Pike of the think tank GlobalSecurity.org. "You don't see a lot of lobbying going on for the defense budget because everybody knows who's got the contracts." But the new homeland-security budget, he adds, is another matter. "For specific sectors and specific companies, it's going to be generating a feeding frenzy. It already has."[11]

Many Washington observers would argue that such relations in the midst of security and military operations are far less likely to receive the sort of political scrutiny by Congress or other stakeholders (e.g., the media) than has been the case elsewhere. Others argue that the security imperative trumps the unavoidable potential for abuse that is nonetheless limited by ongoing government controls and processes: as homeland security matures, goes this line of thought, so will the oversight capacities to handle discrepancies and malfeasant behaviour.

In Canada, much less is known about lobbying practices in the realm of public safety and security,[12] yet it is a safe bet that the orientation of technology and consulting service companies has responded in kind. Beyond the implications for lobbying, the rising importance of security and antiterrorism efforts by national governments also carries important implications for business and government interactions in such a context — in jointly safeguarding increasingly networked forms of infrastructure and in acting collaboratively in both policy and strategy.

Shared Accountability

For the private sector, the political dynamics of security and privacy are central to the business calculus of managing shareholder and stakeholder relationships. A leading business advisory body in the United Kingdom outlines the separate and shared responsibilities of business and government in such an environment: "The call for a more purposeful Government role in no way relieves business, individually and collectively, of their duty to customers, shareholders, employees and society as a whole to make information assurance a high priority, to raise their own standards of protection, and to cooperate in every way with Government. Corporate executives should be held accountable by shareholders and, ultimately the law, if they fail to provide adequate security and to motivate vigilance, compliance, and initiative throughout their companies. Businesses must become more ready to share information about threats and incidents with one another and with government" (IAAC 2002).

This last line is not without controversy and resistance, however, a point underscored by Google's ongoing efforts to shield information about Internet searching from the US federal authorities. Although the particular legal challenge against Google deals not with antiterrorism but with efforts by the federal government to better track pornographic activities involving children (an uncontested aim), the principles of consumer privacy (shaping Google's reputation in the marketplace) as well as concerns about proprietary product information have dissuaded Google from complying to US government demands (despite the widely held view that some of its main competitors, including Yahoo and Microsoft, have relinquished similar information holdings, refusing to publicly confirm or deny such action).

In this manner, the heightened state of alert and expanded antiterrorism efforts of US government authorities often complicate the relationship with industry. The US strategy for cybersecurity developed by the federal government, for example, relies heavily on public sector–private sector cooperation, a priority significantly bolstered over the past few years within the realm of overall homeland security efforts.[13] At the same time, companies such as Google face difficult choices about the nature of corporate and consumer privacy and how best to navigate what can be conflicting stakeholder pressures.

Internet companies are not alone. In May 2006, *USA Today* fanned what perhaps had been a flickering flame of controversy pertaining to the federal government's NSA wiretapping of international phone calls (in a manner circumventing traditional channels of judicial approval and congressional oversight). The story involved alleged information requests made by the federal government of leading American telephone providers that pertained to customer calls, both foreign and domestic. Once again, most companies refused to deny the allegations (though congressional investigations appeared inevitable).

In early June 2006, the *Washington Post* reported highly fractious meetings between industry and government officials on the generalization of policy and procedures pertaining to the holding and transferring of information between the two sectors. In August, the federal courts would rule the NSA wiretapping program unconstitutional, ordering its immediate disbanding, action that is pending appeals by the Bush administration that will likely necessitate consideration by the US Supreme Court.

The case of Choice Point underscores both the opportunity and the risk for the private sector. A leading gatherer and processor of information — providing services such as background checks and credit reports to clients such as financial, insurance, and market research companies, Choice Point would become a strategic ally of the US federal government in its post-9/11 security efforts, assisting federal agencies in trolling through the billions of data files potentially accessible in today's digital universe, "mining" such data pools for patterns or identifiers of suspicious conduct (O'Harrow 2004). The company would also become the focus of a widening probe of its own handling and sharing of information and whether actions breached domestic privacy laws. Widely criticized in media circles and online blogs, punished with the largest privacy-related fine ever administered in the United States, the company continues to operate while mounting a defence of its policies and actions.[14]

In light of Choice Point and related cases, the aggressive legislative stance by the State of California (home to many of the country's leading technology companies) suggests an increasingly adversarial environment between sectors. Yet tougher regulatory and criminal capacities at the federal level may not only conflict with the strategic aims of the government to work more collaboratively with private sector specialists but also generate intensive lobbying efforts by various industries and special interests (a theme discussed in chapter 2). In the United States, the public is increasingly onside with the need for new and tougher laws on matters of privacy and information protection (Scalet 2006).

For Canada, such issues, while slower to emerge in the public realm, are gradually becoming more prevalent. Prior to the 2006 federal election, the then Liberal-led cabinet had introduced before Parliament new legislation that would have considerably augmented the government's ability to monitor e-mail traffic as well as the requirements of private companies to provide the technical capabilities necessary to satisfy the demands of government watchers.

The issue arose publicly in July 2006 in an unwelcoming manner for Bell Sympatico, the country's largest Internet access supplier. Leading Internet policy expert Michael Geist summarized the case on his blog:

> Canadian Internet users were abuzz last week with reports that Bell Sympatico, Canada's largest Internet service provider, had opened the door to increased customer surveillance through changes to its user agreement. While Bell denied that the amendments were linked to the so-called "lawful access" initiative that may require ISPs to install new surveillance technologies, the furor associated with the story highlights Canadians' mounting concern with their online privacy.

The Bell clause, which took effect on June 15th, advised subscribers that the company retains the right to "monitor or investigate content or your use of your service provider's networks and to disclose any information necessary to satisfy any laws, regulations or other governmental request."

Few doubt that ISPs already monitor network usage and will disclose subscriber information, including usage habits, if required to do so under a court order. The new clause raised fears, however, that Bell was extending that scrutiny to the active monitoring of user content as well as escalating its willingness to disclose subscriber information without prior judicial oversight.

For its part, Bell swiftly issued a statement emphatically denying that the amendments were linked to lawful access, maintaining that the company had "a long and established history of protecting the privacy of its customers."

From a political perspective, last week's incident is only the latest example of significant public outcry when the lawful access proposals attract attention from the mainstream media. Over the past year, there have been a growing number of editorials cautioning against legislation that would increase Internet surveillance yet decrease judicial oversight. Notwithstanding public sentiment against new surveillance, successive governments seem determined to revive the lawful access proposals. The Liberal government introduced a bill mandating new surveillance requirements late last year, and the Conservatives are expected to introduce similar legislation this fall.

If lawful access legislation re-emerges, the fallout is likely to extend beyond the political arena to the network providers themselves. Five companies — Bell, Telus, Rogers, Shaw, and Videotron — presently dominate the Canadian high-speed residential Internet market. These companies regularly maintain their commitment to protect their customers' privacy through accessible privacy policies, open communications with customers, and a willingness to resolve privacy disputes should they arise.

Yet that may not be enough. As Canadians react to the lawful access proposals, many will want to see network providers supporting their privacy interests. To date that has not occurred; since those same providers have been perceived to be more concerned with the financial costs associated with lawful access (the Ottawa rumour mill suggests that the Conservative government will commit tens of millions of dollars to the lawful access program to address those cost concerns).[15]

Another dimension of shared accountability between business and government stems from the outsourcing activities of many governments in Canada (and elsewhere) resulting in functions previously undertaken within the confines of public sector organizations shifting to external specialists delivering that function via a contractual partnership. As explained in the previous chapter, outsourcing entails the transfer of technical and organizational resources (often including personnel) to this external provider, and in the realm of digital technologies this type of collaborative activity has become engrained into the fabric of organizational life. The Province of British Columbia has entered into a number of such arrangements in recent years; accordingly, many components of the information management architecture within the province rely increasingly on the direct involvement of private companies, and in many cases these companies invariably handle personal data pertaining to citizens of British Columbia.[16]

In 2004, the provincially appointed privacy commissioner of British Columbia publicly declared that such information could be at risk of being directly sought by American authorities due to provisions of the Patriot Act. The concern stems from the fact that many companies involved in outsourcing activities in the province are, in fact, Canadian subsidiaries of US corporations. Thus, these companies could be obliged in some instances, according to the commissioner (an independent office of the BC legislature), to share their information holdings with US authorities if called upon to do so (due to invocation of the Patriot Act for a security-related matter). Despite efforts by government officials at all levels in Canada to downplay the significance of this issue (which nonetheless received considerable media coverage), it was subsequently revealed that internally officials in the federal government confirmed the BC privacy commissioner's view.

Although legal experts dispute the reach of the Patriot Act in facilitating information gathering in Canada, the significance of any such "threat" is mitigated by two complementary vehicles: contracting provisions (limiting the actions of American companies working with Canadian governments), and a more implicit protocol of goodwill between the two countries that renders such subversive action not only risky (in generating a public backlash) but also less efficient than other means of bilateral cooperation to ensure that the informational needs of both countries are being looked after. Seeking to minimize public concern and government intrusion, the head of the Information Technology Association of Canada underscores this latter point: "Regarding the controversy around the US Patriot Act, the ICT Industry believes strongly that it would be inappropriate for US law enforcement authorities to try to obtain personal information on Canadian citizens from an outsourcing contractor....In fact, US authorities have established arrangements in place with Canadian authorities and there should be no difficulty in obtaining such information for any legitimate anti-terrorism investigation purposes by going through Canadian authorities to get the information at the source" (Courtois 2005, 5).

Geist (2005) argues that, while legal challenges were unsuccessful in blocking the deal, the courts did explicitly open the door to prospective or actual privacy breaches as a legitimate means of challenge. Indeed, what ultimately insulated the deal across both legal and political purviews were the subsequent steps undertaken by the company and the provincial government to bolster contracting provisions protecting information while adding significant financial penalties for any breach should one occur.

Geist (2005) argues that the BC case marks the beginning of a third stage of Canadian privacy law — one likely to feature tougher rules and enforcement by guardians. In contrast, the first stage encompassed a largely self-regulatory approach orchestrated by the Canadian Standards Association in the early 1990s. The second, current phase included initial legislative action such as the 1998 federal statute on privacy protection that came into effect in 2001 (the Personal Information Protection and Electronic Documents Act). Here the preceding voluntary guidelines became mandatory requirements for most forms of commercial activity with a "light" regulatory model emphasizing mediation and non-binding investigations by the federal privacy commissioner.

The new laws have required companies to inform customers about how their information is being handled, to seek consent before sharing such information, and to allow individuals the right to access and review any information held (similar but separate rules cover public sector authorities). The first formal review occurred in 2006. Geist (2005) summarizes three currents of what he envisions as a forthcoming third and much more stringent phase of privacy regulation:

> First, as frustration mounts over the Commissioner's lack of order making power as well as the policy of shielding the targets of privacy complaints, the third stage of privacy law will feature growing pressures to address these issues through a statutory amendment.
>
> Second, with the avalanche of privacy breach disclosures involving data companies such as ChoicePoint, the next stage of privacy law is likely to include the uniform adoption of legally-mandated disclosures of privacy breaches.
>
> Third, the BC outsourcing case points to the need for increased statutory protections for personal information that may secretly be disclosed to foreign law enforcement authorities.

Tougher regulations and laws within specific jurisdictions, however, cannot suffice in a world where commercial and terrorist activities increasingly transcend the legislative scope of any single country. The complexity of the security imperative is compounded by the difficulties of orchestrating collective action transnationally.

Beyond National Borders

According to Weber (2005), two resulting and conflicting notions of a border lie at the heart of an emergent open-source political economy. He envisions the twenty-first century as a clash of hierarchy and networks, a comparison that can be applied not only to the world of software development (e.g., Microsoft as the proprietary champion versus open-source alternatives) but also to the traditional democratic governing bodies and structures of countries (organized primarily in a hierarchical manner) and more networked communities of economic, social, and terrorist actors. These latter movements not only reject hierarchy and control but also transcend traditional notions of national space and boundaries (Ferguson and Jones 2002).

An additional risk on a global scale is the increasingly secretive and centralized manner in which the Internet itself is being managed (Zinnbauer 2004). Here too the United States is a focal point of tensions between unilateralism and technological prowess and the view by most other countries that some form of multilateral system of governance for the Internet is required (Drake 2004).

The issue has further exasperated global tensions surrounding current US control over the main Internet servers, with even the European Union abandoning the American position at the November 2005 World Summit on the Information Society, the second phase of this UN-led initiative designed to broker a new global compact on the governance of the Internet and the world's increasingly shared telecommunications infrastructure (Hermida 2005). The face-saving compromise included a pledge to empower a UN body to further study the issue and recommend solutions, a move that the US federal government insisted would not alter existing arrangements (justified primarily on security grounds).

Weak multilateralism, coupled with the explicit efforts of countries such as China and Singapore to censor online behaviour, does not lend unequivocal support to the notion of a borderless world. Politically, national governments remain key actors in global governance forums as well as central figures in the policies and rules of Internet access and usage within their own countries. These political structures have implications economically since, while there are a few large multinational corporations that have arguably transcended their reliance on any one home country, most industries and companies remain most directly concerned with policy and regulatory issues within their domestic environments, interacting with and lobbying their governments accordingly.

The Internet and the widening global digital infrastructure of telecommunications are continually fuelling challenges and threats that require policy responses and governance mechanisms that transcend national boundaries. Naim (2006) underscores this point in lamenting the US debate pertaining to immigration and physical border controls (e.g., the proposed construction of a security wall along the southern border) and the detachment between national polities, new technologies, and integrating economies:

> Yet the paradox of policing borders in a high-tech, globally integrated era is that today, less sovereignty may equal more protection. In order to reinforce national boundaries and combat terrorism, one of the most effective tools a government can deploy is collaboration with other nations—in effect, ceding or "pooling" certain aspects of their sovereignty.
>
> That is no easy task. It requires partnering with less efficient, less democratic and less trustworthy nations and sharing information, technology, intelligence and decision-making power. In many quarters—Washington and beyond—the notion of diluting national sovereignty verges on treason.... But when threats travel via fiber optics or inside migrating

birds, and when finding ways to move illegal goods across borders promises unimaginable wealth or the only chance of a decent life, unilateral security measures have the unfortunate whiff of a Maginot line.

The resulting dilemma is whether national authoritative structures—established primarily to address the interests of domestic constituencies, can be accompanied by transnational mechanisms with both the clout and the capacity to elevate the public interest test to the global level or at least to regional levels. Doing so entails not only the pooling of sovereignty that Naim and others seek, as to some degree this is happening covertly and informally, but also making such international collaboration visibly understood and accountable to an enlarged polity.

Until now, the principle of privacy has mainly been construed as an individual right administered within national legal and political structures. The term is also analogous to how countries view national sovereignty as a basis for their own form of political privacy with respect to information sharing and competing national interests: information may be shared when necessary but certainly not freely. Indeed, a likely outcome of the Arar Commission is the imposition of stricter protocols on the ability of Canadian law enforcement and security authorities to share information with their American counterparts.

Such a reaction is understandable from the perspective of the rights of Canadians, but it may not be preferable in the context of addressing common security threats and movements whose origins and actions are not bound by the logic of national borders. As the case of Arar so vividly illustrates, more cooperation cannot occur if unaccompanied by some measure of openness and oversight—at the least within each democratic jurisdiction but increasingly over time between them as well. The present conundrum remains the increasingly transnational scope of privacy and security matters that fuel interdependence and the mainly national-centric policy arenas and Boulding triangles within which governance systems remain firmly entrenched.

CONCLUSION

With respect to the interrelations between business and government, the security imperative carries many points of relevance for each of three relational templates examined at the outset of this book. First, the commercial and guardian syndromes can exert separate influences on matters of security as objectives and risks vary in each case. For companies, underlying motives of profit and new opportunity mean that privacy and security considerations must be weighed against potential gains to the consumer such as convenience, better service, and increased competition. Governments, in contrast, face a different calculus in executing a broader set of guardian functions that defines the public interest balance between personal freedom and privacy on the one hand and collective security on the other.

Within Stanbury's policy arena, the clashing of these partially unique sets of motivators and interests invariably leads to tensions and attempts to exert influence. Lobbying on security matters is thus increasingly prevalent as companies attempt to keep the guardians at bay with respect to new rules and regulations while also seeking to exploit new opportunities in augmenting the public sector's organizational and technological capacities to combat terrorism and other threats.

The heightened security imperative also underscores, however, the converging interests of business and government in facing what amounts to a set of interdependent prospects for a sustained balance of commercial growth and opportunity on the one hand and stability and security on the other. The digital infrastructure that underpins today's service-oriented and increasingly online economy is the same one that enables governments to repackage their public service offerings while also trolling the vast oceans of information holdings for breaches, breakdowns, and threats. Neither sector is up to this task alone, and both sectors face grave consequences in the event of failure.

To face today's security and privacy challenges, organizations from both the private and the public sectors must demonstrate a capacity to balance commercial and guardian traits within their own confines. Companies must balance shareholder value with varied stakeholder interests, obligations that create both conflictual and collaborative ties within the marketplace, while governments, in effectively pursuing their guardian orientation, must act nimbly and creatively, often in concert with private companies, to respond to dispersed and dynamic threats. In sum, the collective security agenda intensifies the interdependence between business and government and the corresponding importance of collective learning.

CHAPTER FIVE

INNOVATION AND DEVELOPMENT

INTRODUCTION

The previous chapter concluded by examining how the security challenge transcends any single country despite the predominance of national systems in many aspects of governance (particularly that of the public sector). This chapter begins by extending this transnational lens to the realm of innovation, since the globalization of markets coupled with technological connectivity creates a widening canvas for developing and sharing ideas. As with security, however, the tentative emergence of a global system of innovation faces significant governance obstacles, since the regime of intellectual property rights, the basis of incentives and protections for inventors, has traditionally been maintained by guardian mechanisms at the national level. A key reason why strengthening global governance is such a difficult challenge is that countries compete with one another to exploit economic advantages and maximize prospects for domestic development. The diverging interests of the developed versus the developing world are particularly acute, and countries such as China and India often resist new rules, tacitly favouring piracy that enables an influx of new products and knowledge, key to underpinning the growth of knowledge-based industries. New technologies that allow for multinational supply chains and research and development networks further complicate this equation, as it is no longer easy to equate the interests of a globally minded company with a single country.

At the same time, despite rising commercial mobility and connectivity, development patterns in most countries retain an important commonality—namely, the importance of proximity and localizing spaces within domestic borders. Much as China is evolving into an economic network of sophisticated and powerful urban centres, mixing public infrastructure and private ingenuity, a similar dynamic is unfolding in North America and indeed around much of the world. Accordingly, a key dimension of this chapter is the localization of relations between business and government: cities and communities can and must be viewed as distinct jurisdictions with their own governance systems involving business, government, and, importantly, the community and the civic sector. Drawing primarily on the prism of the Boulding triangle, this third sector is particularly prominent locally given the nexus between territorial proximity and socioeconomic activity and association.

Key lessons in this regard can be drawn from California's Silicon Valley, widely viewed as a governance microcosm of an innovation and network-driven economy. As innovation systems and information flows become increasingly dispersed around the world, Silicon Valley personifies how a local space can remain a critical venue for relations between business, government, civic organizations, and the citizenry. Here the collaborative imperative can represent a form of collective advantage (or handicap) for a city or community competing with other locales. I then examine both Canada's innovation geography through this urban-rural lens and the implications for the growth prospects and stakeholder engagements of companies. Politically, whether local governments are up to the task of orchestrating good governance within their jurisdictions is also a key variable of the importance of place in today's world, one intertwined with the multilevel governance tensions of a political federation such as Canada.

CONNECTIVITY AND PIRACY

For much of the twentieth century, economic development as processes of both production and redistribution could be understood primarily through the prism of national governance and a workable balance between commercial and private interests on the one hand and guardian and public interests on the other. Elevating any such balance is both complex and contested: the schism between commercial integration and security considerations pursued mainly through a public interest defined nationally is a case in point. So is the absence of global consensus and the resulting variance in national approaches to creating and respecting intellectual property rights (IPR). The issue is particularly acute in China, where some widely cited estimates place the software piracy rate in excess of 90 percent (Wang, Zhang, and Ouyang 2005).

Yet, while piracy fuels Chinese growth across many manufacturing industries, it has done so mainly in low-value, low-cost, commodity-type goods (a category that can often include software programs designed elsewhere). The dilemma for China is that, as it seeks to move up the global value chain by fostering more endogenous innovation, especially in technology- and knowledge-intensive sectors, there are growing calls from within as well as outside the country for strengthening IPR to safeguard economic incentives for innovation and nurture bottom-up clusters of entrepreneurial companies (Eger 2006). China's entry into the World Trade Organization (WTO) is viewed as an important enabler in this regard by integrationists who are hopeful that wider trade and economic interdependence will foster a convergence of policy and legal principles despite obvious differences in political ideologies.

Indeed, these transitional parameters of economic and marketplace-based activities are threatening to paralyze and outdate traditional trade-oriented forums such as the WTO (formerly the General Agreement on Tariffs and Trade [GATT]). As tariffs decline the world over (though most significantly in the developed world[1]), a host of non-tariff barriers pertaining to national regulatory regimes around issues such as intellectual property rights are creating new tensions between countries, not only between developed and developing nations but also within these groupings. A 2006 episode involving American pressure to convince the Swedish government to change its laws pertaining to online copyright enforcement is illustrative,[2] as it created a bitter political backlash in Sweden and some unease between Europe and the United States, which traditionally view one another as global allies with respect to such debates.

Alongside the WTO and its IPR affiliate, the World Intellectual Property Organization,[3] are other sources of emerging dialogue on new matters such as the governance of the Internet itself, another divisive issue where the American preference for the status quo (i.e., its own control over Internet servers and a high degree of influence over the body governing online traffic[4]) is facing growing resistance from both developed and developing countries that are calling for a new multilateral structure. A 2005 Summit on the Information Society held under the auspices of the United Nations ended in short-term gridlock, with all sides agreeing to examine future scenarios and a reiteration by the US federal government that it has no plans to relinquish its control over the Internet anytime soon.

With respect to intellectual property rights, UN agencies and bodies such as the OECD have begun to devote more time and study to the matter, much as the WTO and WIPO continue to make efforts to further strengthen and align an IPR regime across member countries (fewer in the case of WIPO than the WTO). Moreover, the private sector is beginning to mobilize its interests and voice internationally, elevating in some manner the traditional interplay of business and government influencing dynamics (i.e., those examined in chapter 2) from the national plane to the global plane.

One such example pertaining to software piracy is the efforts of the Business Software Alliance (BSA), a global federation of technology companies that ties together affiliated national and panregional bodies from around the world. With respect to software piracy, the BSA commissioned a study by IDC Research claiming that, globally, a 10 percent decrease over four years in the current piracy rate of 35 percent would create 2.4 million new jobs, $400 billion in economic growth, and $67 billion in new tax revenues for governments.[5]

Although surely it is not coincidental that China and Russia are highlighted as having the most to gain from effective IPR enforcement, such efforts illustrate recognition within the business sector that sustaining globalization requires a capacity to address issues on a worldwide scale. Yet, in an acknowledgement of the current structures of political authority, the five major recommendations put forth in the report (creating strong legal protection for IPR, increasing enforcement, targeting resources, improving public education and awareness, and setting an example through government leadership) are all aimed at bolstering the capacities of national guardians.

In the absence of a global authority to administer IPR (an absence of sufficient guardian capacities, to invoke once again the language of Jacobs), the present environment is characterized by (1) bilateral efforts to resolve specific issues (e.g., the US-Swedish case or American efforts to qualify Russia's pending WTO membership with promises to address lax IPR enforcement in Russia); (2) complex and very gradual multilateral dialogues across existing institutions involving competing national interests politically accompanied by private sector interests that are in some cases consistent with national affiliation while in other cases separate from it via more transnational industry bodies; and (3) a growing set of underground activities determined to transcend current political and legal arrangements.

The last trend is itself complicated by the fact that while some elements are indisputably illegal (e.g., the most aggressive forms of individual and organized crime), others are more contested not only by specific criminal interests but also by more mainstream movements from industry and civil society whose preferences pertaining to IPR issues vary widely from those of companies seeking rigid enforcement. The music industry and the rapid rise of online file sharing are the most pronounced examples of a mainstream division between legal rules and those seeking to establish what might be termed a new behavioural ethos that can blur the distinction between blatant illegal action and new economic and social challenges motivated by competing claims of how to balance effectively private and public interest considerations.

In Canada, these competing tensions have been evident in recent debates on and changes to public policy. The Canadian node of the aforementioned BSA network, the Canadian Alliance Against Software Theft (CAAST), estimates losses stemming from software theft to be in excess of $1 billion annually; it is just one among many groups from cultural and communications sectors that have pressured the federal government into tightening IP rules and enforcement in the country. Concerns about growing copyright infringement fuelled lobbying efforts that led to the then-Liberal government's tabling new legislation in 2005 containing a new package of measures designed to mandate Internet service providers (ISPs) to gather and provide consumer-user data to government authorities. In the United States alone, over 16,000 individuals have been the recipients of legal action pertaining to music downloading as of early 2006, action for which the sort of ISP-gathered information is an important prerequisite.

In parallel, many private sector copyright holders have begun to deploy so-called digital rights management (DRM) technologies as a means of better tracking and controlling access to and usage of their creations. DRM is thus a new form of surveillance in the public realm aimed at better respect of private interests. Welcome by some (especially those who fear violations of their IPR), such tools nonetheless face a backlash due to the sorts of privacy concerns discussed in the previous chapter. The recent SONY BMG case is instructive in this regard, and Canadian groups such as intellectualprivacy.ca are aligning with privacy commissioners and other critics in charging that an overly effective IPR regime, especially one making use of new technologies, may come at a great cost in terms of not only freedom of expression but also freedom of learning and the erosion of personal privacy rights. The views of Supreme Court Justice LeBel have been put forth in support of such concerns: an individual's surfing and downloading activities "tend to reveal core biographical information about a person. Privacy interests of individuals will be directly implicated where owners of copyrighted works or their collective societies attempt to retrieve data from Internet Service Providers about an end user's downloading of copyrighted works. We should therefore be chary of adopting a test that may encourage such monitoring."[6]

While such cross-currents exist within each country, the resulting complexity for global commerce is heightened because different countries may have competing interests in terms of how they address such issues both within their own jurisdictions and across them. Legal principles that are foundational in Western societies may be shunned or tacitly ignored in other cultures. Consequently, globalization and the central dynamics of innovation at the heart of new economic opportunities for much of the developed world are unfolding across a patchwork of national IPR models (themselves in flux and rigidly maintained to varying degrees) that fall well short of a stable system of market governance with the requisite balance between commercial and guardian capacities. The resulting challenge is twofold: first, convincing countries to create and enforce agreed-to IPR mechanisms within their own borders; second, creating some basis of effective governance globally to mediate between national differences and disputes and to foster a more integrative IPR regime for a globalizing marketplace.

At the other end of the geographical spectrum, this mobility of knowledge and information and the circumventing of many traditional forms of national control have done little to quell the importance of traditional geographical proximity in terms of how innovation is organized and conducted. Although countries are the key units politically in responding to the transnational dilemmas of piracy and the like, increasingly cities and subnational regions encompass the critical learning synergies of clustering, research, and social networking. In short, much as Naisbitt (1994) envisioned, one paradox of globalization is the reinforced importance of smaller spaces and systems in an increasingly open and interdependent world.

COLLABORATION AND PROXIMITY

The process of innovation that is now central to wealth creation in most societies has evolved in a manner that is highly interwoven with multiple sets of governance factors that are at once local, national, and transnational. Locally, an environment of what economists term "shared externalities" nurtures (or stymies) innovation. Whether these externalities are positive or negative depends on (1) the existence and actions of interrelated companies clustered with one another; (2) supportive research institutions bridging longer-term research and development (R&D) geared to short-term commercialization opportunities; and (3) a surrounding set of civic and community actors conducive to both creativity and collaborative action (Storper 1997; Roy 1998).

While there are many national factors that shape these localized systems (once again positively or negatively), the importance of territorial proximity to the nurturing of formal and informal linkages across these various elements is an inherently localizing dynamic that most often favours urbanized settings where companies, public and private research institutions, and more abundant and diverse workforces and civic organizations are most likely to agglomerate and interact with one another.

California's Silicon Valley has long been regarded as the poster child for such local prowess in terms of aligning commercialization, creativity, and innovation, particularly in the twin engines of the so-called new economy, computer hardware and software and digital content services on the one hand and life sciences and biotechnology on the other. With respect to digital industries, the region is home to global flagship companies such as Cisco Systems, Hewlett Packard, Yahoo, and Google, to name but a few. In the realm of life sciences, some of the leading companies include Varian Medical, Roche, Gilead Sciences, and Genencor.

In 2004, the region's productivity rate was reportedly 31 percent higher than the US average, and its present endowment of not only companies and research bodies but also entrepreneurial support systems has become a reference point for all cities and regions seeking development opportunities in a knowledge-based, innovation-driven economy: "Silicon Valley provides a special habitat for innovation and entrepreneurship. It consists of dense, flexible networks and relationships among entrepreneurs, venture capitalists, university researchers, lawyers, consultants, highly skilled employees, and others who know how to translate ideas into new commercial products and services fast enough to stay on the edge of the innovation curve. These complex networks continually connect people to good ideas and test the changing market, always searching for the next innovation."[7]

Also important is that the nexus between these two broad industrial and innovation streams (within which many subclusters can be identified[8]) is expected to be a major source of new economic activity in the years ahead: the convergence of biotechnology, information technology, and nanotechnology represents Silicon Valley's newest cluster with widening commercial and research activities devoted to it. Accordingly, while Silicon Valley is not without its challenges (a theme returned to below), resulting in periodic musings (from both outside and within the region) about an uncertain future, the region has remained on the leading edge of technological innovation since the advent of computer systems in the twentieth century.

If Silicon Valley is the United States' most powerful proxy for its innovation and technological strength, a model studied by cities and regions everywhere, it is also a reflection of the opportunities and difficulties confronting this country as it becomes increasingly integrated economically with other parts of the world. In addition to Saxenian's efforts, the region's own analysis confirms the levels of interconnection between local clusters and global business and innovation networks:

> Like other regions, Silicon Valley must find a role to play in a global economy that has become a series of "value chains" connecting product design, flexible production, marketing, and logistics functions. This is a complex process involving many partners across numerous locations throughout the world. Today, the region's firms increasingly rely on their Silicon Valley workforce to make specific, high-end contributions to these global value chains — focusing on tasks such as "creative" product design, innovation services, business management, and the like. At the same time, many companies have outsourced and "offshored" other functions to lower-cost locations in order to remain globally competitive enterprises. As products increasingly become commodities and production becomes routine, the competitive advantage of high-cost regions depends on the ability to add value in new and creative ways. Silicon Valley's competitive edge is its ability to create new ideas, methods, product designs, services and businesses based on its engineering, science, and management expertise. (JVSVN 2005, 52)

Two points from this quotation are noteworthy: first, the acknowledgement that regions such as Silicon Valley are high-cost locales and therefore compete on a different basis and for different economic niches than lower-cost regions that may be located elsewhere in the United States but that increasingly are likely to be found in developing countries; second, the growing reliance of local companies on production chains that are ever more global, shifting much of the traditional manufacturing and low-skilled jobs base elsewhere, leaving behind an intensifying need for creativity and innovation.

The first point reinforces the collaborative, learning premium of good governance within high-cost regions (a category that includes most urban centres in North America) that must search for ways to, if not replicate or displace Silicon Valley itself, at least foster a set of local conditions in terms of quality of life that will attract the most highly skilled and the most mobile segments of a national and global workforce. This point is the central thesis put forward by Florida (2002) in his examination of the nexus between this new "creative class" and the quality of life attributes of American cities, a template that has since been imported into Canada to examine similar dynamics among Canadian cities (Bradford 2003). Such findings accentuate the prospects for an urban-rural divide, due to the intensity, diversity, and correspondingly more creative institutional environment of the city (Friedmann 2002).

Within Silicon Valley, collaboration has been shown to be a key strength of the region's resilience (Wonglimpiyarat 2005). This horizontal integration of both the marketplace and the regional workplace is a key aspect of the entrepreneurial networking that underpins the region's identity. In many cases, workers are said to be loyal less to a single company than to the region as a whole, with job mobility a traditional and much more enshrined workplace pattern there than elsewhere (a point of distinction lessening as the knowledge economy has spread its roots). This "ecosystem" of positive interdependence that drives the valley extends beyond the market sector to include supportive research institutions, notably Stanford University, particularly adept at fostering an entrepreneurial culture conducive to business outreach and collaborative research activity (Saxenian 1994).

Similarly, the term "civic entrepreneurs," in reference to supportive community initiatives and non-profit enablers of not only public-private interactions but also broader community visioning and engagement, stems primarily from Silicon Valley pioneers and the foundational and ongoing efforts of its flagship civic entrepreneur, Joint Venture Silicon Valley Network (JVSVN) (Henton, Melville, and Walesh 1997).[9] Civic entrepreneurs are thus an important catalyst of social capital—the lubricant for collaborative networking both within the marketplace and between companies and across sectors (Putnam 1994; Patterson and Biagi 2003). Social capital exits, however, comprise a complex phenomenon based on many factors, such as local history and tradition, market and legal structures, and public policies that either encourage or mitigate collaborative behaviour (Westlund 2005). In Silicon Valley, the vibrancy of immigrant communities is one such example: many Chinese Americans, shunned for promotion by the subtle discriminatory practices of large technology companies in the 1970s and 1980s, formed their own ventures instead, often relying on ethnic-based associations to nurture, finance, and grow new enterprises (Saxenian 1994).

This regional co-evolution of interests and players is a good personification of the learning culture encompassing sectoral collaboration and mutual adjustment, as depicted by Paquet's presentation of the Boulding triangle (Paquet 2002; Paquet, Roy, and Wilson 2004). The actions of JVSVN-like organizations and the levels of business engagement in such endeavours also lend support to the interdependence between shareholder and stakeholder relations as well as the strategic and territorial importance of the latter for most companies. The annual "regional index" produced by this organization is a proxy for the identity of regional governance that transcends any single local government or community but nonetheless bases its efforts on the collective boundaries of this regional entity with an unmistakable and globally recognized identity (Paquet, Roy, and Wilson 2004).

In light of considerable internal threats facing the region, in particular high costs of housing and land and environmental degradation of both the natural and the transportation infrastructures (with traffic congestion a particular concern), the response of companies and private entrepreneurs has not been to flee Silicon Valley (as some observers have long predicted) but to engage in collective efforts to strengthen the performance of the region, mitigating (though certainly not eliminating) the endogenous weaknesses that threaten the valley's attractiveness relative to other locales both within and outside the United States (as civic leaders from cities and regions around the world routinely attempt to attract individuals and organizations from the valley).

A revealing aspect of the valley's evolution in the twenty-first century is how its growth is tied to both the aforementioned governance strengths and a workforce and an immigrant community that are at once global and local. Saxenian's most recent research, for example, dispels any notion that China and India (two important sources of human capital within Silicon Valley) are threatening the sustainability of the valley as a creative and innovative region. Instead, networks of transmigrants are becoming more common in facilitating greater levels of interdependence and shared growth between people and places across these jurisdictions. The result, according to Saxenian (2002), is a reformulation of the traditional notion of "brain drain" to one of "brain circulation," in which mobility and interlinkages not only between countries but also across specific cities and regions become simultaneous sources of creativity and growth for multiple locales.

Even as Silicon Valley is a uniquely powerful laboratory of collaborative governance locally (increasingly tied to globalization), its historical development and ongoing prospects are also shaped by national governance variables. Two types of resources are particularly interwoven with national institutions and business-government relations at this level: intellectual capital and the protection of property rights on the one hand and human capital and immigration flows on the other.

In terms of intellectual property, and perhaps the most widely regarded indicator of new IP generation, new patents, Silicon Valley's commercial and innovation strengths are once again evident. In 2005, the valley accounted for nearly half of all new patents granted in California (itself the leading state), a figure translating into eleven percent of all new US patents awarded. Here is what many observers regard as creative tension, or "coopetition," between the open and collaborative ethos of the valley, which encourages knowledge transfer and professional and social mobility, and efforts by researchers and companies to register and seek protection for their inventions (Capello 1999; Keating, Loughlin, and Deschouwer 2003). Such protection is a critical enabler of future profit streams, as a return on what can be significant upfront R&D efforts and costs, since competitors are limited in deploying the same methods in their own products and services (unless licensed to do so, representing a compensating revenue stream for the inventor).

Researchers in companies and laboratories are often rewarded on the basis of new patent development, much as large companies are becoming increasingly aggressive in pursuing patent infringement claims via legal proceedings. It is nonetheless notable that Silicon Valley's success is owed at least in part to an unusually liberal attitude internally with respect to IP management, by Stanford University, that negotiated much more freely with researchers and corporate partners in sharing IP rights and resulting revenue streams than had typically been the case in the United States or elsewhere (Saxenian 1994). In short, Silicon Valley couples local openness and collaboration and a concerted effort at IP generation and usage with a global reliance on an IP regime based on recognizable and enforceable rules.

With regard to human capital, Silicon Valley's tremendous attractiveness to skilled workers from around the world (and emerging economies such as China and India in particular), coupled with its California setting and corresponding reliance on Hispanic migrant workers, makes it a unique venue and voice in debates about immigration, especially in a post-9/11 environment. In fact, nearly 40 percent of valley residents were born somewhere other than in the United States (JVSVN 2005).

Prior to 2001, technology interests in the valley led lobbying efforts in Sacramento and Washington aimed at more liberal immigration policies nationally and more welcoming policies at the state level, especially for Hispanic workers most at risk of marginalization in the high-skilled, high-cost Silicon Valley locale (President Bush's open-mindedness to Mexico and immigration reform in the 2000 election was welcome in Silicon Valley). More recently, immigration backlash and political fixation on border security have been viewed ominously by many in Silicon Valley concerned about attracting and retaining migrant workers. Ongoing lobbying efforts by valley companies and regional trade and civic associations were viewed as an important factor in securing a commitment by the president in his 2006 State of the Union Address to reform immigration policy and accommodate the needs of highly skilled, research-intensive sectors and regions (Sperling 2006).

As a result of this changing social and political context, due to its technological prowess and abundant research infrastructure, many companies in Silicon Valley find themselves engaged in new sets of both collaborative and adversarial relations with federal government authorities (of the sorts examined in preceding chapters). Silicon Valley and its media-intensive neighbour to the south, Los Angeles-Hollywood, have thus become central venues in debates pertaining to what many regard as key threats to US security and development in an open and increasingly integrated world: intellectual piracy and rapidly growing segments of what might be termed a digital underground economy that are globalizing in parallel to legal activities.

CANADA'S INNOVATION GEOGRAPHY

With regard to economic growth and the localizing conditions of innovation and entrepreneurship (conditions entailing close strategic collaboration across business, government, and the community), Silicon Valley has long been a reference point for regions of all shapes and sizes in most countries, and Canada is no exception. For instance, one of the earliest and most influential of such efforts, Coté's *Growing the Next Silicon Valley* (1987), attempted to extract the inward-networking logic of endogenous innovation and community-based adaptation as a means of reframing traditional industrial policies, formed and implemented in a largely top-down manner, into a more bottom-up perspective on local and regional development.

The results in Canada from the public sector perspective have since been mixed, with both federal and provincial governments proving to be more than a little schizophrenic about the relative merits of devolving power locally (Paquet and Roy 2004). Such hesitation from above stems from a mixture of more narrow forms of bureaucratic and political resistance to relinquishing power and its accompanying resource base to more complex and cyclical debates concerning themes such as innovation, security, and connectedness that have, in recent years, ushered in a resurgence of the nation-state as the most important governance prism.[10]

With respect to systems of innovation, for example, the term was originally deployed to reflect countries as such systems, particularly those with small geographies and relatively homogeneous populations (e.g., those of middle and northern Europe). As researchers examined innovation policy and relational patterns in North America, the following became evident.

1. National governments played an important role through a variety of policy instruments aimed at business promotion and industrial regulation, science and technology research, and regional and community development.
2. The provinces (or states in the United States, Australia, etc.) mirrored much of these activities within their own jurisdictions.
3. In keeping with Coté's aforementioned recipe inspired by Silicon Valley, local proximity and both interfirm and intersectoral networking mattered greatly in fostering endogenous growth opportunities by linking research, commercial, and civic interests in manners best suited to localized conditions. (Patterson and Biagi 2003; Slack, Bourne, and Gertler 2003; Scott 2004)

There has since been widespread recognition that Canada's governance environment has long been out of balance with respect to national frameworks and top-down directions on the one hand and bottom-up, localized dynamics on the other, excessively weighed down by the former at the expense of the latter. Yet, despite such weaknesses, the advent of local innovation and surrounding governance systems, encompassing the commercial clustering and civic engagement dynamics so visibly central to Silicon Valley's success, has imposed itself across the country, and those studying the geography of innovation do so today with a firm eye on local and regional variants and conditions for success (de la Mothe and Paquet 1998; Donald 2005; Niosi and Banik 2005).

Yet how such local perspectives have emerged within a top-down setting of federal and provincial resources, structures, and actors has accentuated the emergence of three distinct geographical categories of innovation and endogenous development. They are (1) Canada's three largest cities — Toronto, Montreal, and Vancouver — and their immediate metropolitan surroundings, (2) small and medium-sized cities; and (3) rural and remote communities.[11]

Although there are important differences between all three groups, the most distinct cleavage — the pronounced urban-rural divide — falls between the first and second categories of urbanized dwellings and the remaining rural constituencies. The handicaps that plague rural communities are varied and the focus of much study, but they can generally be summarized as three main sorts of deficiencies: political clout, innovation base, and technological infrastructure. All three deficiencies are closely intertwined with a nexus of demographic and market forces that further reinforce what some view as not only an urban advantage but also a disadvantage for countries not sufficiently urbanized (Institute for Competitiveness and Prosperity 2004).

Despite excessive political centralization provincially and federally, with respect to innovation the economic handicap for cities and industrial clusters congregating within them is partially lessened by the reality that most mid-sized Canadian cities are also political capitals of provinces. The importance of government presence is often a key variable in explaining the emergence of Silicon Valley–type clusters, intensely tied to research and creativity, as displayed by Ottawa's telecommunications prowess, Toronto's significant endowment of provincial research and infrastructure spending (and the proximity of public and private sectors as a result), and the emergence of St. John's as Newfoundland and Labrador's best hope for knowledge industries and new economic activity (either abandoning the traditional resource base or integrating it into new economic pursuits).

There are, of course, regional exceptions to this pattern (Kelowna, London, Saskatoon, Regina, Moncton, to name but a few), but even here such centres are not without significant public sector underpinnings, particularly those involving innovation resources.[12] Indeed, an important lesson of the geography of research and commercial activity in the twenty-first century is that the innovation capacity of a locality involves important mixes of public and private activity, as even Silicon Valley itself has been shown to be greatly aided by such a marriage.

Canada's three largest metropolitan areas and their population diversity distinguish them as innovation environments. The potential for a strong innovation advantage is tied to many of the attributes of Silicon Valley examined above, which are more likely to be found in cities: chief among them are the tendency of clusters to congregate close to an innovation infrastructure predominantly urban and a sufficiently skilled workforce. This latter point is accentuated by Saxenian's brain circulation and Florida's nexus between urban diversity, immigration, and creativity. A city such as Toronto, one of the most culturally diverse in the world, can thus benefit accordingly, offsetting the high costs of big-city living with the tangible and intangible benefits of proximity and quality of life.

Yet the notion of big-city attractiveness is not assured and is a central focus of economic development planners and civic boosters alike. Two key issues stand out, both threatening to erode such premiums. The first issue is that immigrant inflows may be not only a question of choice but also an act of perceived necessity by new migrants seeking ties to ethnic communities found predominantly or exclusively in large cities. Such inflows include both skilled and unskilled workers, and the challenge for a city (and for a country by virtue of national immigration and cultural policies) is thus to minimize barriers to education, upward economic mobility, and civic engagement.

The social cohesion of larger cities is accordingly under strain due to different patterns of success among social and ethnic groups (much as Silicon Valley's Chinese and Indian migrant communities are shown to be faring much better than less wealthy and less educated Hispanic workers and families). Similarly, this economic and cultural diversity across an expansive urban area (i.e., the City of Toronto and the Greater Toronto Area) may impede the efforts of civic entrepreneurs and local governments to mobilize and sustain sectoral partnerships — given the tremendous complexity of identities and institutional arrangements (Gertler and Wolfe 2002).

The second issue that threatens quality of life in the largest cities is the escalating, multifaceted costs of urban congestion — including unaffordable housing, traffic gridlock, air and noise pollution, to name but a few. Here the size and scope of Canada's "megacities" pale in comparison to how such a status is accorded globally, but the sustainability of large urban economies is an increasingly acute challenge, one that grants opportunities for mid-sized cities to distinguish themselves by blending less intense levels of urbanization with nonetheless a significant degree of economic and civic diversity. Those close to the largest urban centres (e.g., those surrounding but separate from the Greater Toronto Area, including areas as far west as London) may well be in a position to benefit from spillover effects rooted in cost and quality-of-life advantages.

For many other entities, however, the challenge of new immigrant concentration is becoming a significant concern, for the risk is that only the largest and most culturally diverse of Canada's cities are able to foster the sorts of human interdependencies and innovation dynamics ascribed by Saxenian and Florida. While exceptions present themselves (Alberta's full-employment economy is a powerful draw for new immigrants to cities there), a province such as Nova Scotia has now formally recognized insufficient immigration as a key barrier to future growth, particularly for the metropolitan capital of Halifax. Accordingly, within the province, this urban emphasis has not gone unnoticed by civic leaders in Cape Breton who fear immigrant concentration in Halifax at their expense, leading to questions about subprovincial autonomy and growth of the provincial capital at the expense of more peripheral regions (Patterson and Biagi 2003).[13]

Much as immigration intensity thus seems to favour the largest cities, others assign a form of collaborative advantage to mid-sized cities that may be better placed to form more cohesive identities and wider community engagements. A proven determinant is the ability of such centres to create and nurture a sufficient degree of economic diversity (a factor often taken for granted in the largest cities), which, in her previous works, Jacobs showed to be the central ingredient of urban resilience and growth. Canada's Technology Triangle (enjoining Kitchener, Waterloo, and Cambridge in southwestern Ontario), for example, is a highly diversified economy, blending new economic sectors spun out of area universities with significant segments of financial services, automobile assembly and parts suppliers, and agricultural and rural equipment manufacturing, to name but a few.

The area's shifting but sustaining patterns of diversity have been ascribed to a uniquely vibrant local culture of civic leadership and commercial entrepreneurship that is both a historical and a contemporary success factor for this region (Roy 1998). These sorts of dynamics have been uncovered elsewhere in Canadian locales of a similar scope, where Bradford (2003) stresses the interplay of seven key aspects of community-based innovation: (1) local champions; (2) institutional intermediaries; (3) equitable participation; (4) a creative civic culture; (5) financial and technical resources; (6) robust accountability mechanisms; and (7) indicators to benchmark progress.

Although no one area is shown to be comprehensively successful at nurturing all such aspects, Bradford's review of a "second tier" of mid-sized cities and regions in Canada and elsewhere reveals an endogenous premium on private and public and civic actions nurtured primarily from within as opposed to a top-down imposition by external forces. In a related commentary, Bradford (2004) emphasizes the political handicap facing Canadian communities from an absence of sufficient local and intergovernmental capacities to nurture such dynamics compared with Europe, where a community and regional emphasis is much more engrained in the institutional fabric of the European Union and many of its member countries.

The consequences of such a handicap are particularly severe for the smallest communities, mainly rural and often far from the largest cities and provincial capitals. Three sets of variables call into question the feasibility of many such settlements:

(1) the declining natural resource base of many single-industry towns and regions;

(2) the aforementioned nexus between urbanization and innovation and related consequences for broadband infrastructure; and

(3) an excessively centralized government sector for the country as a whole prepared to make limited interprovincial financial transfers at the cost of structurally impeding stronger potentials for localized responses within the communities most at risk.

One important study of rural prospects conducted in the United States but nonetheless relevant to Canada concluded that localized creativity and adaptation must be coupled with a significantly reformed and devolved set of policy and governance frameworks that empower communities with the resources and the tools to identify and pursue new clustering opportunities in self-identified niche areas (Porter et al. 2004).

From the vantage point of the private sector, the first objective of businesses is establishment and survival. Companies are generally far less mobile and fleeting than their workforces, but central to expansion and new business creation is a sufficient pool of entrepreneurship both within existing companies (characterized in the past as intrapreneurship) and with an eye on creating new ones. Here individuals and companies making choices for risky entrepreneurial pursuits are likely to view positively a high degree of mobility and networking, as in Silicon Valley (Cohen and Fields 1999).

The corresponding set of collaborative conditions across the public and civic institutional spheres determines the extent to which workforce development and human capital strategies (including attraction and retention) are an asset or a liability for local performance (Maskell 2000; Montana et al. 2001). In the absence of a strong mixture of private, public, and civic capacities, businesses face stagnation, and regions face a higher likelihood of socioeconomic exodus.

In this regard, the systemic weaknesses of local governance in Canada from the perspective of the public sector, a point highlighted by both domestic and international groups (e.g., the OECD in the latter case), can become a serious impediment to growth and prosperity (OECD 2002). Hubbard and Paquet (2006) echo such concerns, pointing to the inertia of the public sector as a critical vise on innovation in all spheres of governance, thereby threatening future competitiveness and prosperity. Such concerns have resulted in a growing voice, particularly across urban communities. Important research undertaken by TD Canada Trust on the future of Toronto and urban areas (in separate but related studies) has helped to spur important calls for a devolution of fiscal powers to local authorities, calls that have since shaped reform discussions both locally and nationally.[14]

Other civic groups, such as the Conference Board of Canada, have further accentuated the emphasis on local dimensions to economic innovation and development and governance reforms more generally, coupling more traditional national economic reporting schemes with regularized metrics of individual cities, for example. In terms of corporate governance, community thus becomes a key stakeholder for individual companies, not only as a recipient of responsible behaviour and philanthropic activity but also as a strategic base of competitive and collaborative networking; these are important dimensions of performance and ultimately the value generated for shareholders.

Yet, despite this growing movement of localization, many of the actions and much of the attention of companies devoted to public affairs may gravitate to federal and provincial governments in light of the larger sets of both resources and rules that they hold. How the public sector is adapting to the increasingly global and local forms of socioeconomic activity and technological connectedness is the focus of the next section.

SMARTER COMMUNITIES AND FEDERATED CAPACITIES

The challenges facing municipal governance systems and formal bodies of local government are twofold. First, the distribution of identities across national, provincial, and local planes may well be shaped by patterns of resources and visibility that inherently favour national authorities. Second, there may be tensions and differences between geographically defined communities on the one hand and the formal municipal authority on the other — meaning that localized communities may be strengthening in a manner that is largely disconnected from municipal institutions (Amin 1996; Andrew 2002). These challenges are interrelated and further complicated by the advent of a digital world and the overlapping formation of virtual communities.

The danger is that a weak public sector locally means diminished representation of public interest matters as partnering across commercial and guardian organizations evolves. The corruptive dangers of corporatist-style lobbying are greater due to weakened participative capacities involving both companies and citizens that are the foundations of localized learning, adaptation, and accountability. Ironically, while provincial and federal governments continue to struggle with questions of organizational competence and political legitimacy, there is reason to believe that citizens would welcome a greater devolution of power to municipal and local authorities (Commission on Legislative Democracy 2004). Public opinion polling by the Centre for Research and Information on Canada, for example, reveals a considerable decline in trust levels accorded to provincial and federal governments and much higher trust levels accorded to municipal bodies.[15]

Over the past two decades, many of Canada's largest cities — as well as a number of smaller communities — have witnessed political amalgamations underpinned by the common objective of both simplifying and unifying municipal governance.[16] Efficiency and clarity were often the guiding principles of such exercises — designed in many cases to replace multitiered systems with single councils and an elected mayor to oversee a strengthened municipal administration. What may well have been sacrificed in this movement is more creativity in devising local capacities for self-governance and adaptation, thereby further distinguishing local democracy and government from provincial and federal levels. The risk is that democracy here becomes grassroots and engaging and more hierarchical.

The City of Toronto is a case in point: forty-four elected councillors (in addition to the mayor) serving a population of roughly 2.5 million comprise an image more in line with provincial legislatures than a "local council." Although officially non-partisan, what is increasingly parliamentary about such a body is the growing professionalization of a political class that must, of necessity, act more indirectly for their constituents than would have been the case under previous models of multitiered local governments.

Moreover, as with the recent evolution of federal and provincial forums, the concentration of power in the mayor's office, although not as absolute as that of a prime minister or premier in majority, is an important feature of many cities — a principle aspired to by many of those designing the new models put in place.[17] The City of Toronto is not unique, however, as urban centres such as Ottawa, Gatineau, Calgary, Winnipeg, and Halifax are but a few governed by a single council with a relatively small number of elected officials for a growing and diversifying population.[18]

Here Silicon Valley has also been an important reference point, albeit one more contested for its political virtues and limitations. During the debates that preceded the imposition by the Province of Ontario of a single-city government in Ottawa (across what had been the two-tiered regional municipality of Ottawa-Carleton), proponents of amalgamation argued strenuously for a wider and stronger public sector perspective on growth and governance not only for individualized communities, some urban and some rural, but also for the metropolitan entity as a whole (some going as far as extending this logic to the National Capital Region [Paquet, Roy, and Wilson 2004]). In this view, the civic and resulting social and fiscal fragmentation of the broader Ottawa area required a sufficiently political body with the powers and accountability to steer the region forward more strategically and holistically.

Skeptics of such a path invoked Silicon Valley as a model of the virtues of a plurality of local government systems, more flexible and less bureaucratic, competing with one another but also collaborating when necessary via new civic partnership models such as Joint Venture. The technology community in Silicon Valley has never called for single, enlarged government — fearing, according to this camp, greater rigidity and less influence and responsiveness. In reality, the geocomplexity of Silicon Valley, extending from the Bay Area of San Francisco to its de facto capital, San Jose, calls into question the feasibility of any such single structure, but the point remains — is one larger government better than a network of smaller ones?

Those in favour of amalgamation made a persuasive case that, with respect to the specific attributes of Ottawa, an affirmative response makes the most sense. Indeed, the social and civic weaknesses that Silicon Valley leaders themselves report on, including ethnic and social polarization, an overly stretched transportation infrastructure, and environmental degradation, demand a strengthened public interest dimension to planning and governance processes. While cities such as Ottawa are thus better equipped formally to chart a regional course, the struggle continues to balance such a capacity with community activism and multiple forms of democratic and business engagement found at the grassroots level (Paquet 2002).

With respect to the prospects for more digital forms of democracy, the conundrum here is that without a stronger degree of importance attached to self-governance from the local perspective, any such effort will be visibly overshadowed by national and transnational challenges and processes (Roy 2006b). It may even be the case that expanded sets of provincial and federal initiatives — without an underlying municipal component (and some careful thought about how to align democratic participation across all government levels) could further erode municipal autonomy and identity.

Ontario's pursuit of e-health reforms offers a parallel lesson of sorts. Here the creation of Local Health Integration Networks, in order to foster community engagement and stakeholder collaboration, has been managed closely by a provincial government struggling to reconcile system-wide change on a provincial scale and the need for localized learning and experimentation (Roy 2007).

The emergence of the Internet and virtual communications is an important prism through which the new style of governance arrangements may be identified and crafted, as organizations in all sectors seek to foster coordination in a manner that reconciles central authority and flexible autonomy: such is the notion of a federated architecture that is as much political and organizational as it is technological. Indeed, the scope of what must be sought is explicitly multidimensional: technically, it permits decision-making systems within a variety of organizational subunits to join together; strategically and politically, it allows for both action and authority to be facilitated, shared, and coordinated across a multitude of levels and activities (Koch 2002).

An optimistic reading of this new, federated, and digital geography of innovation and creativity is that opportunities are created to enjoin the traditional advantages of proximity with globalizing processes facilitated by information and human mobility (leading to the brain circulation and global embeddings of Silicon Valley and many like-minded cities). The dangers, however, are twofold: first, questionable public sector capacities both within and outside the traditional national space; second, a widening cleavage between places that are well endowed and typically urban and smaller and mainly rural communities that risk further marginalization. Effectively mitigating such risks is unlikely to emerge through a reliance on market forces alone; also needed are fostering and aligning commercial, guardian, and civic capacities to do so.

The emergence and evolution of broadband infrastructure as primarily an urban phenomenon illustrate this point with respect to bridging the urban-rural divide (much as a similar logic applies to how a global digital divide reinforces polarizing tendencies between developed and developing worlds). Even within urban centres enjoying strong market offerings, local governments are leading efforts to forge new wireless infrastructures through public-private partnerships that serve as a hybrid approach in bridging the commercial model of Internet access as a private good with a view that online connectivity is at the same time becoming a form of public good (i.e., a basic necessity and/or necessary enabler) where the costs of market exclusion are high.

For rural and the smallest of communities, limited state and civic capacities make the formation of such partnerships much more difficult (as the public sector's leverage is reduced accordingly). Here is where the logic of a federated architecture must entail an alignment of bottom-up efforts with the support and strategic assistance from other levels of government (through direct involvement with local stakeholders as well as the setting of broader regulatory frameworks that shape industry incentives and constraints). Countries that are overcoming the limited geographical tendencies of market forces and closing their own digital divides more rapidly than is the case in the United States and Canada have done so through such a balance (Chen and Wellman 2003).

CONCLUSION: LOCAL EMPOWERMENT FOR GLOBAL SUCCESS

An important lesson to be derived from this chapter is that, as traditional notions of place are increasingly challenged, the world of business-government relations now entails a governance architecture that is increasingly federated across many levels both within and beyond national borders. Locally, moreover, the nexus between proximity, innovation, and commercialization coupled with the embedding of most businesses within the strengths and weaknesses of their immediately surrounding communities makes stakeholder engagement and collaborative forms of governance strategic imperatives. In response to their global positioning, however, cities and communities must also couple inward forms of multisector engagement with an outward connectedness that stimulates diversity, creativity, and innovation.

Such a challenge is interwoven politically with public sector capacities that encompass provincial and national dimensions. As long as federal and provincial governments dominate the resource and regulatory landscape, the key policy arenas for influence will also be there. The resulting question for municipal governments is whether their operational and political capacities are sufficient in orchestrating multistakeholder venues and collaborative developments. A problem remains: rising disenchantment with and disenfranchisement from senior-order governments are not being coupled with a more local democratic and participatory renaissance. A consequence is that collaborative ties between industry and government, and the fusing of public and private interests into partnership arrangements involving civic entrepreneurs, are more likely to remain technocratic and specialized, of interest to key sectoral leaders but off the radar screen of the typical citizen.

Corruption remains an extreme risk of such limited engagement, although such cases of malfeasance remain more exceptional than normal practice, much as their exposure has yielded important remedial action. More pervasive and corroding, however, is a deepening of the socioeconomic cleavages that are now symbolized by the digital divide. For large cities, economic and cultural diversity may well suffice to nurture growth—but the absence of a strong public sector matters given public interest dimensions to quality of life and the inclusiveness of the civic fabric that are viewed as critical generators of social capital (with networking repercussions for business and market entrepreneurship). For the smallest of communities, weak public sector capacities mean limited tools and efforts to spur new development, reinforcing dependence on senior-order governments. With the continuance of urbanization, many provinces exhibit a negative mixing of both these trends.

For business and government, the essence of the social learning challenge for cities and communities is to collaborate to effectively navigate and cultivate the shared space within a localized Boulding triangle—in a manner that seeks opportunities from global connectedness. The local partnering that must occur between sectors must in turn be accompanied by not only political oversight but also the widest possible levels of public engagement. Such conditions are necessary to ensure both enlightened distinctions between the commercial and guardian interests called for by Jacobs and the co-evolutionary adaptation espoused by Paquet. In sum, localized learning and global connectedness are intimately interrelated.

CONCLUSION

THE NEED FOR VIRTUOUS HYBRIDS

Despite the emergence of a more socially, technologically, and organizationally networked world, the messages put forth by Jacobs, Stanbury, and Paquet with respect to sectoral relations remain useful guideposts. Business and government continue to be fundamentally different in both purpose and structure, they continue to influence and attempt to influence one another on matters of policy and strategy, and they continue to be intertwined in shared governance models and processes that impact themselves as well as their jurisdictions as a whole.

As discussed in the introduction, the guiding premise of this book has been that these three typologies are not at odds with one another; rather, they can be viewed as complementary lenses through which the growing amount of networked interaction between public, private, and civic sectors can best be understood. Fundamentally, Jacobs' boundaries create the conditions for lobbying as well as many of the challenges for multisectoral collaboration. While the Boulding triangle boundaries must certainly be transcended — and often renegotiated (a key thematic lesson of Paquet's work) — erasing or ignoring such boundaries can only lead to a dangerous path of ineffective governance arrangements at best, corrupt and harmful ones at worst.

At the nexus of today's sectoral interactions, there are two overriding and interrelated commonalities that affect the three sectoral typologies examined throughout this book. They include the widening emphasis on (1) transparency and more direct forms of both participation and accountability and (2) a language of stakeholder engagement and sustainability-driven governance systems. As the preceding chapters demonstrate, the relative strength of these trends is not uncontested by variables such as tradition, varied interests and objectives (across sectors and countries), and rising degrees of complexity across most realms of society.

Growing demands for transparency and direct accountability permeate concerns and discussions pertaining to corporate governance in the private realm and democratic governance in the public realm. Both along with and beyond calls for proper oversight and challenge functions by boards and legislative committees respectively, shareholders and citizens are becoming less passive and deferential — seeking to become more informed and involved in shaping decisions and directions. Similarly, within organizations, the same logic is reflected in less hierarchical and more networked, horizontal work patterns, personified by companies such as Google that provide their knowledge workers with the means and flexibility to create and collaborate.

Transparency is a precursor to such involvement both internally and externally. Yet it is not without its challenges as both corporations and governments may often feel as though accelerating external information flows (emboldening activists and citizens alike) call for a more tightly orchestrated message from within. This tension between a command-and-control mentality rooted in clarity, decisiveness, and top-down authority on the one hand and more consultative and collaborative styles of decision making on the other is at the heart of the twenty-first-century nexus between management, leadership, and governance (Rheingold 2002; Reid 2004; Paquet 2005; Roy 2006b).

Such tension also pervades governance challenges of a more encompassing or systemic variety involving multiple sectors and how they interact. For instance, the traditional world of lobbying — secretive and often outside the realm of formal structures and rules — is gradually giving way to what was described in chapter 2 as legitimacy-based lobbying. This perspective does not seek to negate the self-interest, competitive motivations of private corporations that often clash with public interest, and more collective demands; rather, it places a higher ethical standard on more open intervention (which also creates the conditions for at least the possibility of compromise as a basis for consensus and learning when multiple interests and viewpoints collide).

This view of lobbying as a legitimate and overt business function carries the potential to transform the adversarial and linear policy arena described by Stanbury while also challenging Jacobs' inspired notion of stark boundaries between business and government as somehow optimal. Such stances mean that only a select few — professional lobbyists with privileged points of access — can transcend sectoral boundaries. Increasingly, however, organizations in all sectors face situations of interdependence, and as a result companies must do more than contract lobbyists to act on their behalf: they must act on their own behalf.

Acting in this manner, more directly and openly in arenas and processes that transcend sectoral boundaries, brings us closer to Paquet's co-evolutionary world inspired by the Boulding triangle. In such a world, multistakeholder governance is understood to be not only necessary and workable but also optimal. While this language of "stakeholders" is relatively common in the public sector, many firms in the business realm remain suspicious of the term (Adams and Frost 2003). Despite widespread discussion and reform pertaining to corporate governance, relatively few North American companies overtly acknowledge stakeholder relations, although the proportion of companies doing so is rising (Stratos 2003).

More subversively, however, despite reluctance to explicitly embrace the term "stakeholder," its meaning and impact are widening through a range of philosophically aligned concepts: corporate social responsibility and ethically conscious institutional investing are cases in point. What enjoins these practices are social and ecological variables that constitute a basis for sustainability as the focal point of good governance in the twenty-first century. The imposition of climate change as the centrepiece of a renewed focus on environmental policies and sustainable governance capacities could well be the defining prism of multisectoral governance for the years to come (Innovest 2002).

Indeed, the climate change challenge is instructive. Paquet's co-evolutionary language adopted within the context of the Boulding triangle fits well with the ecological dimension to planning and decision making for both organizations and societies as a whole. The commonality is interdependence, as professed by those who warn of the perils of climate change: atmospheric conditions, water temperatures, animal migratory patterns, and conditions for human development are all intertwined; the same is true for individuals, organizations, and institutions, all coexisting within a governance architecture for a given jurisdiction (Paquet 1999). The systemic challenge for creating sustainable governance is resilience through learning and adaptation, the scope of this challenge now increasingly global for humanity as a whole (Glenn and Gordon 2006).

At the same time, sustainability as a principle encompasses more than ecological sensitivity — denoting the ability of jurisdictions to adapt to change and to flourish over an extended period. Threats to this continuance may be ecological, but they may also be technological, economic, and social. Silicon Valley, for instance, as reviewed in chapter 5, has long struggled with a variety of social ills — affordability and crime and poverty tied to educational polarization and social exclusion — that threaten to erode the region's ability to continually attract and retain the new talent required to sustain growth.

These distributional issues within this regional microcosm of the knowledge economy that is Silicon Valley are also playing out both nationally and globally. Some studies of global wealth patterns estimated that by the year 2000 more than half of all assets were owned by just 2 percent of adults, while the top half of this select group themselves controlled 40 percent of all assets. This growing polarization of wealth and opportunity has similarly been cast in the technology-inspired depiction of the digital divide, a multifaceted divide that likewise exists within countries and communities as well as between them.[1]

Such globalizing dimensions to growth and distribution have galvanized efforts by global bodies and private sector actors to view sustainability as a collective challenge that emphasizes both shareholder return and stakeholder responsibility (and their interdependence). While market forces and the commercial traits of entrepreneurs and investors dictate that profit undoubtedly remains the key imperative of private corporations, what matters here is a growing recognition that such profit can be sustainable only if business is a partner in forging the global conditions necessary to sustain market activity and the support of civil societies in allowing markets to function.

A key question for transforming sustainable governance principles into multisectoral partnerships and concrete actions rests with the capacities of the state sector to mobilize beyond national borders. In the absence of stronger global institutions, the present situation dictates that companies will focus primarily on lobbying national political actors who, in turn, seek to safeguard their national interests in the international realm. Even the European Union, with a transnational political base on which to build, has so far seen its efforts to create a continental market for carbon emissions trading flounder due to the national inertia of industrial and political interests primarily presented and pursued in national terms (Neuhoff and Grubb 2006).

Yet few would disagree on the importance of creating a market for trading credits based on greenhouse gas emissions — a market estimated to likely grow from infantile trading levels of $10 billion in this decade to annual levels surpassing $50 billion in the foreseeable future (Innovest 2002). This deployment of market forces for a public interest purpose is a useful illustration of why global and national interests rest on the ability to transcend sharp categorizations of commercial and guardian syndromes. Both are called for, and, notwithstanding the complexity of doing so, workable solutions on climate change and other complex issues will be increasingly dependent on innovative governance hybrids enjoining, structurally and culturally, public, private, and civic orientations.

Such hybrids are essential not only to adapting the internal governance arrangements within the Boulding triangle that is typically a country (or a subnational jurisdiction within it) but also to sustaining a conversation between sectors (as stakeholders) about how best to align productively and fairly national interests and needs on the one hand and those of the world as a whole on the other.

The need for virtuous hybrids encompassing multiple sectors is also exemplified by the issue of new national identification mechanisms now being introduced by many countries, including the United States and the United Kingdom. The creation of such mechanisms—involving plastic, wallet-sized cards but also highly sophisticated electronic identifiers, databases, and interoperable systems to process and share information—in turn can be understood as a nexus of many key lessons emerging from chapters 3 and 4 respectively.

Any such mechanism can only be created and deployed on the basis of a combined effort involving both public purpose and private ingenuity. This point is no small challenge, as the UK experience demonstrates: with a spotty track record of managing large IT-based projects with the private sector, the UK government has been extremely concerned about the potential for accelerating costs and administrative quagmires to hamper the realization of this initiative. Unlike jurisdictions such as Scandinavia, where a culture of public-private collaboration is well engrained in the workings of the state, the sort of intimate collaboration required to make the ID project work often remains elusive in the United Kingdom.

Yet there is no alternative but to proceed down such a collaborative path (other than abandoning it completely), since governments have neither the skills nor the resources to create a sophisticated, interoperable identification scheme on their own. Increasingly, the fabric of public sector organizations and their public interest pursuits includes a healthy dose of private sector involvement. The result, as discussed in chapter 3, is that black-and-white dichotomies of market (private) versus state (public) are giving way to collaborative endeavours that blur the boundaries between these sectors. Some have therefore called for a rethinking of the usefulness of such boundaries altogether and the forging of a new space explicitly encompassing overlapping and interlinked public and private dimensions (Andreescu 2003).

This new space finds credence in Paquet's co-evolutionary world, where resilience and adaptiveness are driven by mutual adjustment and collective learning. The difficulty, however, lies in crafting a new space that respects the structural and cultural specificities of markets and democratic arenas respectively. The ideal situation is one where, as Jacobs acknowledged, humans make good use of both moral syndromes (the commercial and the guardian). Does such wisdom imply upholding boundaries and forcing individuals to choose, or does it imply a melding of the syndromes into something more integrative and new?

With respect to the aforementioned example of national ID systems, in those Scandinavian countries where public-private collaboration is arguably the most seamless, there is still an important recognition of the necessity of boundaries and a good deal of separation between those working in private industry and those working in government. Unlike in more corporatist countries such as France, the crossover of individuals between these sectors in the Nordic countries is rare.

In contrast, what is common and central to collaborative undertakings are the constant dialogue between sectors and the transparent settings within which such dialogue occurs. This transparency is due primarily to the high levels of openness in democracy generally and the resulting rules of engagement where companies seeking opportunities with state organizations are concerned. Accordingly, while such openness and dialogue may not facilitate a constant exchange of people, a good deal of empathy and mutual awareness results—a hybrid form of collaborative action that transcends stark commercial and guardian orientations. Such interactivity encourages a stakeholder orientation among companies and helps to ensure that collaborative activities remain accountable to the public by enlightened bodies of political oversight.

By contrast, it seems that the present trend in many other developed countries, especially those of the Anglo-Saxon world, is to seek more aggressively a fusion of public and private interests by either encouraging a select few to move from one sectoral setting to another (typically from industry to government) or forging new organizational entities that are neither purely public nor purely private (e.g., non-profit foundations, joint ventures, etc.). The problem with the first track is that, as noted, the movement tends to be limited and in one direction — with many from the private sector struggling to adjust to an unfamiliar and often unwelcoming world. While often noble in purpose and not without stories of success, such movement cannot suffice to create an expanded, meaningful space for collaborative, virtuous hybrids.

Similarly, many of the new organizational hybrids created often suffer from a perception that they are being established specifically to avoid public accountability. At times, this perception is also the reality — and, as studies have demonstrated, contractual and operational secrecy can often be a breeding ground for mismanagement and ineffectual results (Barton 2006). As discussed in chapter 4, such an absence of transparency can be particularly consequential in the realm of security, where public sector bodies themselves are predisposed to shunning transparency (often with legislative provisions demanding as much). These sorts of conditions dampen pressures for an overt stakeholder culture among private companies; nor do they contribute much to a political and public dialogue that is the basis of social learning.

Within countries, the most promising model of a melding of public and private pursuits may well be found locally, in the form of the so-called civic entrepreneurial organizations discussed in chapter 5. Non-profit in orientation, embedded in a culture of civic engagement, such partnership organizations have proven adept at creating a mix of private resources and ingenuity and public interest pursuits to collectively serve a particular jurisdiction as a whole (most often a territorial community). They are akin to the notion of "gatekeepers," which are central to learning and networking both within market-based clusters of companies and across non-market knowledge institutions (Fleming and Marx 2006).

Notwithstanding the growing importance of virtual communications and exchange, this sort of collaborative networking works best when nurtured by geographical proximity. In the resulting emphasis on the governance of "small worlds," interdependence is viewed as the basis for resilience and innovation (i.e., for sustainability) (Fleming and Marx 2006). In one sense, the small world may be viewed as a miniature version of the Boulding triangle for a region or community and the co-evolutionary dynamics that drive development.

The emergence of a digital infrastructure, rather than diminishing the importance of place, has augmented its importance in terms of intersectoral networking and hybrids as well as the broader participatory capacities of the community as a whole (Roy 2006b). At the same time, however, the notion of place is increasingly contested, much as any localized governance system is intertwined with national and transnational governance systems. Canada's challenge is to mitigate these tensions of a multigovernance world in order to craft an architecture that is suitably flexible in responding to both inward and outward challenges.

CANADA'S ADAPTIVE CHALLENGE

An important challenge for Canada is to foster the conditions for virtuous governance hybrids to flourish. Such hybrids must be grounded in local, provincial, and national contexts and take into account the pressures of extending governance beyond national borders.

Within Canada, the need to bridge the two solitudes of industry and government has been a challenge partially met over the past decade. Industry and government leaders alike routinely invoke the rhetoric of collaboration and partnering, since challenges such as technological innovation and security involve shared externalities that transcend linear sectoral divisions. Furthermore, as such challenges are increasingly tied to competitive and collaborative processes transnationally, agile and effective collaboration between the sectors becomes an important determinant of national performance. This emerging consensus of a governance culture emphasizing market and state (as opposed to one versus the other) was underscored by a recent dialogue initiated by the Public Policy Forum (itself one of many groups devoted to nurturing such a collaborative space).[2]

Yet the challenge remains that this awareness of a new collaborative space has not permeated Canada's governing institutions. Instead, the adversarial mechanisms of parliamentary democracy remain entrenched, and most large corporations continue to prioritize traditional lobbying efforts in the policy arena — partly due to a competitive inertia and partly due to the absence of an alternative governance setting to more forcefully engage corporations and their leaders in new forms of shared governance platforms. The absence of such a new collaborative architecture has been underscored by Hubbard and Paquet (2005, 2006) as a major impediment to improving productivity and prosperity in this emerging century.

Indeed, a case can be made that, since the arrival of the new millennium, Canada has regressed in promoting this collaborative space relative to efforts made in the previous dialogue. High-profile initiatives under both Conservative and Liberal governments during the 1990s, such as the Prosperity Initiative and the Information Highway, brought together leaders from all sectors to define a truly multistakeholder path for key national priorities. More recently, the Liberals reverted to more unilateral efforts on priorities such as the Kyoto Protocol and national security, and the Conservatives have responded in kind, emphasizing personal choice over state control in their childcare plan and market forces as the defining principle of telecommunications reform (largely ignoring a more balanced set of proposals put forth by the Telecommunications Review Panel[3]).

In this regard, there is an important cleavage in terms of the multistakeholder approaches pursued by the public and private sectors respectively. Industry is increasingly active locally, where its own shareholder interests are interwoven with stakeholder considerations that define a community's quality of life, competitiveness, and creativity. At the same time, the private sector is increasingly continentalist and global on matters pertaining to borders, trade, and security — calling for a more aggressive integrationist agenda as a result.

In contrast, the public sector in Canada remains heavily centralized at both provincial and federal levels — to the detriment of local governments as well as more effective territorial-based governance capacities more generally (OECD 2002; Paquet and Roy 2004). With respect to continental matters, despite efforts to characterize the Harper government as more pragmatic about its relationship with its US counterpart, the language of sovereignty remains a *sine qua non* of Canadian politics and prime ministers (especially in a minority government setting in this country and with an extremely unpopular president south of the border).

While many in the private sector would thus prefer — and actively promote — the creation of a de facto Boulding triangle with outer continental boundaries (something akin to the European Union with an initial emphasis on market and security harmonization), the federal government is prepared to entertain such a path only in a tentative and often subversive manner — in large measure due to the underlying skepticism of the Canadian public toward closer continental ties (Roy 2006d).

Such dilemmas are exemplified by the concept of "hollowing out" often invoked somewhat negatively in reference to national capacities (either economic or political) losing ground to forces at once localizing and globalizing. Recent evidence, however, suggests that Canadian companies are flourishing in a world of transnational capital and opening markets, a key driver of growth and prosperity for a country with less than 10 percent of the North American population within its borders (Smith 2006). Yet such success has also been forged on market structures and ownership rules that remain predominantly national, allowing many Canadian companies, such as those in the financial and telecommunications industries, to seek outward opportunities from a domestic position of strength (the major exception here is that of energy, where foreign ownership is more prevalent due partly to the fact that the natural resources driving this industry are territorially, domestically, and literally grounded).

To what degree these national restrictions remain necessary and desirable is a key variable in Canada's development, one that lies at the heart of the nexus between business and government (in a manner underscoring the different relational typologies put forth in this book). For instance, the Conservative minister of industry has actively sought to promote market forces as the main determinant of federal telecommunications policies—even suggesting that in the near future national ownership restrictions may be far less warranted. How market forces (and indeed if) are allowed to unfold from the present arrangements of competitive and ownership policies constitute a major clashing of agendas and interests in this particular policy arena, as familiar rivalries between traditionally telephone-based companies and those rooted in cable television continue to play out.[4]

By the same token, the same government, with the support of the same minister, has introduced new legislation, developed under the guise of national security, to augment the federal government's ability to block foreign acquisitions of Canadian private assets. Here the main concern driving this legislative action is that of China's growing economic clout and this country's interest in Canadian energy and mining companies. One key aspect of concern over China is the high level of state activity in this developing country, with many "businesses" partially or fully state owned. In a sense, then, private competition across opening markets is at times replaced with competition between governance hybrids involving state and industry interests meshed together within one (often national) jurisdiction in a manner that is unrecognizable or ominous in another jurisdiction. This sort of dynamic recalls the 2006 debate in the United States with respect to seaport security and the prospect of a Middle Eastern, state-owned entity being responsible for port facilities on US shores.[5]

Having moved beyond a stark, ideologically laden cold war of market versus state, as well as beyond the free-trade era of tariffs versus protectionism (notwithstanding the notable exception of agriculture), this sort of clash of national (and at times continental) interests and governance hybrids is likely to be the defining element of global competition in this early part of the twenty-first century. The central challenge for countries is to develop a governance order that allows for cooperation and sustainability to be achieved globally through a balancing of international competition on the one hand (competition between companies and countries) and transnational integration on the other (through strengthened regional and international institutions with political authority derived not from direct democratic accountability but from the legitimacy of multistate and multisectoral governance).

Such negotiated action calls not only for an outward extension of the Boulding triangle's boundaries but also for a global dialogue and some agreement on guidelines for sectoral boundaries within such an expanding triangle and the resulting hybrids. As is already the case in Brussels in terms of European Union policies and market structures (and de facto in Washington on many North American matters, chief among them border security), one result is that transnational policy arenas will become more pronounced centres of lobbying and influence. Similarly, with the absence of a global democratic polity, the critical need for virtuous hybrids transnationally is apparent, as the strength and presence of the private sector demand that their roles incorporate elements of both commercial and guardian-minded functionality.

Far from negating the importance of national governance systems, however, these dynamics reinforce the importance of strong and effective collaboration between sectors domestically. The increasingly complex processes of adapting national policies (and sectoral boundaries) to national constituents and agendas and those of a transnational scale dramatically highlight the importance of learning and resilience on a national scale. Here again the absence of a collaborative architecture to steer this country's decision making in this sort of environment is a worrisome handicap.

This outward extension of state and market power also calls for a refocusing of federal government efforts domestically. In his first year in office, Prime Minister Harper has admittedly been surprised by the all-consuming agendas of foreign relations (in contrast to an electoral focus on domestic priorities). Such a surprise is not unwelcome, however, if taken to be a reframing of the national government's role away from domestic comptroller and planner to that of transnational facilitator (and in turn the primary broker domestically among competing regional and sectoral interests). Accordingly, resolving the fiscal disequilibrium among provinces and municipalities in a manner that reduces the administrative scope of the federal government goes hand in hand with building a stronger country that is more prepared and intelligent in its governance-building efforts, both continentally and globally.

The extent to which the federal government is able to lead such a transformation depends on the evolution of Canadians not only as consumers and shareholders in markets and democratic voters but also as civic activists. Already civil society is arguably following the lead of the private sector in becoming increasingly interconnected and focused internationally (e.g., driving both industry and government to take action on environmental matters). The degree to which the basis of a global community takes hold will do much to determine the speed of transnational governance building and the resulting demands placed on countries.

Just as the European Union is struggling to replicate a collaborative culture continentally, which is more commonplace in many smaller EU jurisdictions, so too there may be limits to the extent to which virtuous hybrids can function naturally at the national level in a country such as Canada. In an unfortunate paradox, an excessively centralized public sector at the national and—to a lesser but no less consequential degree—provincial levels means that sectoral boundaries and their preservation are viewed as more important to guard against corruption (and the perceived imposition of subversive forms of collaborative experimentation). Devolution is therefore a necessary but insufficient step: also needed is a more constructive and inclusive dialogue nationally about the importance of intersectoral collaboration and new governance mechanisms to the future of the country as a whole.

The public sector can be an important catalyst for this sort of forward-looking dialogue. A useful model in this regard is Finland's Parliamentary Committee on the Future, a body empowered to undertake futuristic examinations of topics of key interest to Finnish society (often in concert with the private sector and other key stakeholders). In a similar vein, on most key matters of fiscal policy, economic development, and national security (and the governance arrangements associated with such matters), US presidents have long been served by a variety of highly visible and respected multisectoral bodies. While such entities alone are insufficient, they can help to galvanize public awareness and social learning and a basis for coordinated action both within the political realm and across society as a whole.

Embracing and effectively deploying innovative and accountable virtuous hybrids thus require a new national mindset. While differences between business and government must continue to be both recognized and respected, and while overt and adversarial lobbying will continue to occupy an important segment of our democratic polity, it is the nexus of coordination and collaboration among private, public, and civic sectors that will be most important in determining the resilience and adaptive capacities for sustained prosperity in this networked era.

NOTES

Introduction

[1]   A useful review of this book by Professor Mary Ann Glendon of Harvard University is available online at www.firstthings.com/ ftissues/ft9312/reviews/glendon.html.

[2]   The Scandinavian countries (Finland, Sweden, Norway, Denmark) and Iceland are recognized for their transparent governance systems and corresponding lack of corruption. See, for instance, annual surveys completed by Transparency International (www. transparency.org). Indeed, upon assuming the presidency of the European Union in 2006, Finland made greater institutional openness at the EU level a key pledge for its tenure.

[3]   There is no uniform definition of this other sector, which is nonetheless meant to encompass the many forms of formal organizations and informal movements that are neither private sector corporations nor public sector bodies. There are growing numbers of entities and initiatives that reflect hybrids of these various sectors and their governance orientations.

[4]   All of the issues mentioned in this paragraph are revisited in greater detail in chapter 4.

Chapter 1: Corporate Governance

[1]   See Neil Reynolds' column in the *Globe and Mail* of August 16, 2006, "The Untold Story of How Government Got Big," in which Reynolds summarizes the evidence arguing that the expansion of large entitlement programs in this period has solidified spending levels, rendering cutbacks extremely difficult to achieve.

[2]   Various online resources by this author are freely available in text, audio, and video formats at www.jimcollins.com.

3   www.ceocouncil.ca/publications/pdf/5b41c9313b5620ac54ba89d7
    c729fbde/speeches_2002_11_06.pdf, 5.
4   www.msnbc.msn.com/id/12762573/.
5   www.navcanada.ca/NavCanada.asp?Language=en&Content=
    ContentDefinitionFiles\Newsroom\Backgrounders\corporate
    governance.xml.
6   www.calgaryairport.com/document.cfm?did=1326.
7   In 2003, more than 40 percent of all returns were filed online, and
    CRA is a key partner in federal horizontal processes aimed at both
    service integration and domestic security by virtue of its information
    holdings on individuals and organizations.

Chapter 2: Lobbying

1   For the Gomery inquiry into the sponsorship scandal, see www.
    gomery.ca. For the Bellamy inquiry into the Toronto computer-
    leasing scandal, see www.torontoinquiry.ca.
2   See, for example, *National Post* columnist Andrew Coyne's musings
    in his blog, accompanied by readers' reactions: andrewcoyne.
    com/2006/06/canadian-autoworkers-overpriced-sole.php.
3   Source: www.tbs-sct.gc.ca/media/nr-cp/2006/1212_e.asp#bg1.
4   A March 2003 issue of the IRPP publication *Policy Options* (www.
    irpp.org) explored the banking merger issue from a variety of
    viewpoints, including those of industry representatives. Although
    not aimed at the average voter, such an intervention targets the
    policy community responsible for managing such issues within
    the federal apparatus as well as those stakeholders likely to seek
    influence as well (e.g., community groups, small-business forums,
    other financial services organizations, etc.).
5   Abramoff was convicted in 2006 following a plea bargain with
    federal prosecution officials (pleading guilty to federal conspiracy
    and wire fraud charges) that exposed his dealings with numerous
    elected officials, including some close to the leadership of the
    Republican Party in Congress. Abramoff's case is closely linked to
    that of Tom Delay, former leader of the Republicans in the House of
    Representatives, who ultimately resigned his Texas seat in the face
    of mounting legal and political difficulties.
6   Seewww.washingtonpost.com/wp-dyn/content/article/2007/01/
    11/AR2007011102081.html.
7   For instance, the Government of Ontario has appointed a citizens'
    panel to recommend new rules for real-time online reporting of all
    donations made to political parties.
8   www.transparency.org.

[9] www.washingtonpost.com/wp-dyn/content/article/2006/06/20/AR2006062001366.html.

Chapter 3: Procurement and Partnerships

[1] For a useful discussion of Canada's infrastructure gap and the issues and challenges surrounding the usage of public-private partnerships to close the gap, see a June 2006 report produced by TD Canada Trust (www.td.com/economics).

[2] Source: www.pppcouncil.ca/aboutPPP_definition.asp

[3] strategis.ic.gc.ca/epic/internet/inpupr-bdpr.nsf/en/h_qz01586e.html.

[4] For additional details of this and other projects, see www.partnershipsbc.ca.

[5] www.pir.gov.on.ca/userfiles/HTML/cma_4_35659_1.html.

[6] Citing concerns about the ongoing outsourcing initiative between the BC Ministry of Health and Maximus for the management of the Health Insurance British Columbia Program, critics have referred to this report. (An article examining the relationship from various vantage points appeared in the April 2006 issue of *CIO Government Review*.)

[7] Examples include the Municipality of Kingston, Ontario, and Suffolk County in the United Kingdom. Interestingly, the new business model formed by Accenture and BC Hydro (discussed below) is also envisioned to be marketable to other utility organizations (although so far no financial revenue sharing between these parties has been stipulated).

[8] This New York City initiative — though large on a municipal scale — is hardly unique, but it has been recognized as a leading example of such schemes emerging in cities and states across the country. For a complete profile of all the initiatives, see "Effectiveness through E-Payments: Current Learning and Suggested Best Practices," available online at the National Electronic Commerce Coordinating Council (www.ec3.org).

[9] They include customer services, IT services, network computer services, human resources, financial services, purchasing, and building and office services.

Chapter 4: Security and Privacy

[1] See, for example, antichildporn.ca.

[2] The percentage of respondents answering that their organizations experienced unauthorized use of their computer systems (in 2005) increased from 53 percent in 2004 to 56 percent in 2005 (the first

such increase since 2001). The percentage of respondents answering that there was no unauthorized use of their organizations' computer systems decreased over this period from 35 percent to 31 percent (see www.gocsi.com).

3   *EDS Canada Privacy and Identity Management Survey* (2005 white paper), www.eds.com.

4   See www.ornl.gov/sci/techresources/Human_Genome/publicat/ genechoice/glossary.html.

5   Members represent more than $4.5 trillion in annual revenues with combined employment of more than 10 million staff (representing roughly one-third of the total market value of US stocks). See www. businessroundtable.org.

6   Survey details are available at www.csialliance.org/publications/ surveys_and_polls/dci_survey_May2006.

7   www.e-gov.gr/IDABC/2005-10-12.pdf.

8   On repeated occasions, significant portions of government submissions and testimony were censored for "national security reasons." Moreover, the government overruled decisions by the judge leading the inquiry, who argued for the release of information to the public (in some cases, the government chose to black out portions of the judge's rulings pertaining to the information in question). In the spring of 2005, government lawyers argued that RCMP officers should not be compelled to testify (due to national security provisions), and at least one commission advisor went so far as to suggest that the inquiry's findings may never be fully released due to the government's "culture of secrecy" strengthened under the guise of security.

9   See "Government Increasingly Turning to Data Mining," *Washington Post,* June 15, 2006.

10   www.commondreams.org/headlines03/0429-03.htm.

11   www.motherjones.com/news/feature/2002/09/ma_106_01.html.

12   One exception here is media reporting of rising lobbying efforts tied to military operations and pending acquisitions that will result in billions of dollars of new spending. Some reports have claimed that, in pursuing such procurement deals, the government will opt to invoke a national security clause, thereby enabling it to bypass requirements of interprovincial free-trade agreements and impose regional quotas on employment and production for any consortium bidding.

13   Prior to 9/11, the federal government focus on cybersecurity was indirect and fragmented across various e-government and e-commerce initiatives. In February 2003, the president tabled

the country's first ever "national strategy to secure cyberspace," elevating the issue within the executive branch in both the White House and the Department of Homeland Security.

14   For details, see www.privacychoicepoint.com.

15   See www.michaelgeist.ca/content/view/1314/159/.

16   The issue was triggered by the proposal of the BC government to contract out the administration of the province's public health insurance program. In the summer of 2003, the BC Ministry of Health put out a request for proposals seeking a private partner to take over the administration of the BC Medical Services Plan (MSP) and Pharmacare. The province selected Maximus, a private American company with a Canadian subsidiary. The British Columbia Government Employees' Union (BCGEU) then mounted a court challenge to this contracting out. The challenge is a judicial review of the province's decision to contract out based on two grounds: (1) that the contracting out contravenes the "public administration" requirement of the Canada Health Act; (2) that the contracting out violates the BC Freedom of Information and Protection of Privacy Act (FOIPPA). The second ground served as the entry point for the BC privacy commissioner to examine the case.

Chapter 5: Geography and Development

1   Some tariffs and protectionist barriers remain, however, notably in the key sector of agriculture, where divisions between developed and developing countries greatly complicate trade negotiations.

2   In 2004, a Swedish anticopyright organization created a website (The Pirate Bay) devoted to pointing people toward free online IP (nonetheless under copyright protection in one or more countries). As the site did not house any such files directly, it operated on the fringe of Swedish law, attracting many users in that country and around the world. On May 31, 2004, the Swedish authorities shut down the site and arrested its organizers, a move prompted by intense US pressure. A public backlash ensued: within days, the site was up and running once again, albeit from a Dutch source. The site later returned to Swedish operators, and it continues to attract widespread use.

3   "The World Trade Organization (WTO) was established with the successful conclusion of the Uruguay Round GATT Multilateral Trade Negotiations on April 15, 1994. One of the negotiated agreements is the Agreement on Trade-Related Aspects of Intellectual Property Rights (TRIPS), which came into force on January 1, 1995. The TRIPS Agreement brought with it a new era

in the protection and enforcement of intellectual property rights, enhancing the value of WIPO's program of work." See www.wipo. int/about-wipo/en/gib.htm#P52_8261.

4   The Internet Corporation for Assigned Names and Numbers (ICANN) is an internationally organized non-profit corporation that has responsibility for Internet Protocol (IP) address space allocation, protocol identifier assignment, generic (gTLD) and country code (ccTLD) Top-Level Domain name system management, and root server system management functions. These services were originally performed under US government contract by the Internet Assigned Numbers Authority (IANA) and other entities. ICANN now performs the IANA function. As a private-public partnership, ICANN is dedicated to preserving the operational stability of the Internet, to promoting competition, to achieving broad representation of global Internet communities, and to developing policy appropriate to its mission through bottom-up, consensus-based processes (see www.icann.org).

5   www.bsa.org/idcstudy/pdfs/White_Paper.pdf.

6   Background paper by intellectualprivacy.ca, 4.

7   Passage taken from www.siliconvalleyonline.org.

8   The area's seven self-identified strategic clusters include semiconductors, computer and communications hardware, electronic components, software, biomedical devices, creation and innovation, and nano-bio-info technology convergence.

9   A non-profit organization, JVSVN (www.jointventure.org) is a catalyst for collaborative undertakings between technology industries, local governments, educational institutions, and other community groups.

10 Evidence of this point is found in Canada's most recent federal telecommunications policy review examined in chapter 3 as well as the predominant importance of national organizations leading security efforts (discussed in chapter 4).

11 Census data from 1996 published by the Government of Canada point to over 80 percent of the Canadian population living in urban or suburban areas (some 1,720 of 5,984 communities in the country, or approximately thirty percent). More telling is the reality of just over half of the Canadian population found in one of four broad urban regions based on Toronto, Montreal, Calgary and Edmonton combined, and Vancouver.

12 Prominent examples include universities and colleges, federal entities such as the National Research Council, provincial research centres, et cetera.

[13] In 2003 the municipal government for Cape Breton commissioned a study of governance options, including separation and formation of a new province (constitutional matters notwithstanding), the underlying motivation to seek greater funding and operational autonomy from the province based in Halifax. Human capital and innovation resources agglomerating in Halifax is viewed as a barrier to the endogenous prospects of Cape Breton communities facing a decline in natural resources and population outgrowth.

[14] The Province of Ontario is currently creating new legislation specifically for Toronto, designed to augment its decision-making autonomy.

[15] As part of a comparative survey project polling Americans, Mexicans, and Canadians on federalism and different levels and styles of government (in June 2004), only 36 percent of Canadians trusted the federal government to do a good job in carrying out its responsibilities (a decline of 12 percent since 2002). In contrast, 69 percent reported trusting their local governments, the gap between federal and local levels growing by thirty-two points since 2002 (see www.cric.ca).

[16] This characterization applies more to central Canada than elsewhere, as Toronto, Montreal, and Ottawa have all undergone recent amalgamations (while Vancouver has not). Elsewhere, many mid-sized cities, such as Halifax, Winnipeg, and Calgary, either have been amalgamated from previous structures to current unified city models or this latter model has been in place for some time.

[17] The provincially appointed transition boards in Ontario sought to create municipal governance models that vested high degrees of authority and control in the offices of the mayor and the chief administrative officer respectively. Yet, despite parallels to the control exerted by prime ministers and premiers, differences remain by virtue of the absence of formal parties and the need for strong coalition building and persuasion to win council approval.

[18] Vancouver and Montreal remain exceptions with two-tiered variants of municipal governance for the core city and surrounding region, a reality that continues for many of the cities encircling Toronto in the Greater Toronto Area (part of upper-tier regional structures).

Conclusion

[1] In Canada, for instance, the urban-rural divide with respect to Internet access persists across the country. Nova Scotia, for example, has pledged to work with industry to bring broadband service to all communities by 2009.

2   Underscoring this point is a 2006 report on a series of roundtable dialogues with senior officials entitled "The Evolving Role of Governments in a Twenty-First Century Economy." The report dismisses the laissez-faire option of letting markets work and points instead to a more limited variance of views between supportive and strategic public sector roles closely associated with Canadian challenges in a globalizing era. The report is available online at www.ppforum.ca/common/assets/reports/en/report_evolving_ role_of_government.pdf.

3   The panel's recommendations are discussed in chapter 3.

4   On December 11, 2006, the Conservative government overruled prior CRTC market restrictions in opening up most major urban centres to deregulated competition for local phone services: the phone companies responded favourably, while cable companies opposed and vowed to fight the move (prior restrictions allowed telephone companies greater pricing flexibility only after one-quarter of the market share had been taken by alternative service providers, notably cable companies entering this market and fearing predatory-type pricing strategies to keep their efforts at bay).

5   In December 2006, the company at the centre of the controversy, Dubai Ports International, finalized plans to divest itself of ownership of US port facilities to an American investment consortium.

REFERENCES

Accenture. (2006). *Leadership in Customer Service: Building the Trust*. www. accenture.com.

AccountAbility. (2005). *Towards Responsible Lobbying: Leadership and Public Policy*. London: Global Compact.

Adams, C. A., and G. R. Frost. (2003). "Stakeholder Engagement Strategies: Possibilities for the Internet?" Faculty of Business and Economics, Monash University.

AFL-CIO. (2006). *Unchecked: How Wal-Mart Uses Its Might to Block Port Security*. Special Report to the US Congress. www.aflcio.org.

Alexander, C., and L. Pal. (1998). *Digital Democracy: Policy and Politics in the Wired World*. Toronto: Oxford University Press.

Amin, A. (1996). "Beyond Associative Democracy." *New Political Economy*, 1:3, 309–333.

Andreescu, F. (2003). *Post New Public Management Models? New Templates and Possible Lessons from a Commercialising British Public Sector Organization*. Southampton: University of Southampton.

Andrew, C. (2002). *What Is the Municipal Potential?* Regina: Saskatchewan Institute of Public Policy.

Andrews, L. (2006). "Spin: From Tactic to Tabloid." *Journal of Public Affairs*, 6, 31–45.

Archibald, C., C. Galipeau, and G. Paquet. (1990). "Entreprises, gouvernements, et société civile: Une approche co-évolutive," *Gestion*, 15:4, 56–61.

Aucoin, P., J. Smith, and G. Dinsdale. (2004). *Responsible Government: Clarifying Essentials, Dispelling Myths and Exploring Change*. Ottawa: Canada School of Public Service (formerly Canadian Centre for Management Development).

Bakvis, H., and L. Juillet. (2004). *The Horizontal Challenge: Line Departments, Central Agencies, and Leadership*. Ottawa: Canada School of Public Service.

Barton, A. (2006). "Public Sector Accountability and Commercial-in-Confidence Outsourcing Contracts." *Accounting, Auditing, and Accountability Journal*, 19:2, 256–271.

Borins, S. (2004). "A Holistic View of Public Sector Information Technology." *Journal of E-Government*, 1:2, 3–29.

Bradford, N. (2003). "Cities and Communities that Work: Innovative Practices, Enabling Policies." Canadian Policy Research Networks, Discussion Paper F/32.

———. (2004). "Place Matters and Multi-Level Governance: Perspectives on a New Urban Policy Paradigm." *Policy Options*, 25:2, 39–44.

Bryant, A., and B. Colledge. (2002). "Trust in Electronic Commerce Business Relationships." *Journal of Electronic Commerce Research*, 3:2, 32–39.

Burnham, D. (1980). *The Rise of the Computer State*. New York: Random House.

Business Roundtable. (2006). *Essential Steps towards Strengthening America's Cyber Terrorism*. www.businessroundtable.org.

Butterfield, E. (2006). "Northrup Grumman Wins $667 Million San Diego County Outsourcing Deal." *Washington Technology*. www.washingtontechnology.com/news/1_1/outsourcing/27823-1.html.

Capello, R. (1999). "A Spatial Transfer of Knowledge in High-Technology Milieux: Learning versus Collective Learning Processes." *Regional Studies*, 33:4, 353–366.

Cavoukian, A. (2006). *Privacy Guidelines for RFID Information Systems*. Toronto: Office of the Information and Privacy Commissioner of Ontario.

Chen, W., and B. Wellman. (2003). "Charting and Bridging Digital Divides: Comparing Socio-Economic, Gender, Life Stage, and Rural–Urban Internet Access in Eight Countries." AMD Global Consumer Advisory Board, www.amdgcab.org.

Cohen, S., and G. Fields. (1999). "Social Capital and Social Gains in Silicon Valley." *California Management Review*, 41, 108–130.

Collins, J. (1994). *Built to Last: Successful Habits of Visionary Companies*. New York: HarperBusiness.

———. (2001). *Good to Great: Why Some Companies Make the Leap and Others Don't*. New York: HarperBusiness.

Commission on Legislative Democracy. (2004). *New Directions: Public Involvement and Citizen Engagement*. Fredericton: Province of New Brunswick.

Coté, M. (1987). *Growing the Next Silicon Valley*. Montreal: SECOR Consulting.

Courtois, B. (2005). "The US Patriot Act and the Privacy of Canadians." Paper presented at the conference Privacy and Security—Synergies in an E-Society, Victoria, BC, February 11.

de la Mothe, J., and G. Paquet, eds. (1998). *Local and Regional Systems of Innovation*. Boston: Kluwer Academic Press.

Deloitte Consulting. (2005). *Calling a Change in the Outsourcing Market: The Realities of the World's Largest Markets*. New York: Deloitte Touche Tohmatsu.

Dixon, T., G. Pottinger, and A. Jordan. (2005). "Lessons from the Private Finance Initiative in the UK: Benefits, Problems, and Critical Success Factors." *Journal of Property Investment and Finance*, 23:5, 412–423.

Donald, B. (2005). "The Politics of Local Economic Development in Canada's Global Cities: New Dependencies, New Deals, and a New Politics of Scale?" *Space and Polity*, 9:3, 261–291.

Drake, W. J. (2004). "ICT Global Governance and the Public Interest: Infrastructure Issues." Memo 3 for the Social Science Research Council's Research Network on IT and Governance.

Dunleavy, P., H. Margetts, S. Bastow, and J. Tinkler. (2003). "E-Government and Policy Innovation in Seven Liberal Democracies." Paper presented at the Political Studies Association Annual Conference, April 15–17, Leicester University.

Dwyer, P. (2004). "The Rise of Transparency Networks: A New Dynamic for Inclusive Government." In *Future Challenges for E-Government*, ed. J. Halligan and T. Moore. Canberra: Government of Australia. 114–127.

Edelman. (2005). *Edelman Annual Trust Barometer*. Edelman Corporation, www.edelman.com.

Eger, J. (2006). "Can China Let 'A Thousand Flowers Bloom Again'?" *Government Technology*. www.govtech.net/magazine/channel_story.php/100380.

Eggers, W. (2005). *Government 2.0: Using Technology to Improve Education, Cut Red Tape, Reduce Gridlock, and Enhance Democracy*. New York: Rowman and Littlefield.

Ehrenworth, S. (2003). "The Governance of Government." *Optimum Online*, 33:1, 2–9.

European Commission. (2001). *Dependability Development Support Initiative, Conceptual Framework*. Brussels: Information Society Technology Programme.

Fasken/Martineau. (2002). *Corporate Governance Bulletin*. www.fasken.com.

Ferguson, Y. H., and R. J. Barry Jones, eds. (2002). *Political Space: Frontiers of Change and Governance in a Globalizing World*. Albany: SUNY Press.

Fleming, L., and M. Marx. (2006). "Managing Creativity in Small Worlds." *California Management Review*, 48:4, 6–27.

Florida, R. (2002). *The Rise of the Creative Class: And How It's Transforming Work, Leisure, and Everyday Life*. New York: Basic Books.

Friedmann, J. (2002). *The Prospect of Cities*. Minneapolis: University of Minnesota Press.

Fukuyama, F. (2004). *State-Building: Governance and World Order in the 21st Century*. Ithaca: Cornell University Press.

Geist, M. (2005). *The Three Stages of Canadian Privacy Law*. www.michaelgeist.ca/resc/html_bkup/april112005.html.

Gertler, M., and D. Wolfe. (2002). *Local Social Knowledge Management: Community Actors, Institutions, and Multi-Level Governance in Regional Foresight Exercises*. Brussels: Research DG, Directorate K, European Commission.

Gill, M. (2002). *Corporate Governance after Enron and WorldCom: Applying Principles of Results-Based Governance*. Calgary: Synergy Associates.

Glenn, J. C., and T. J. Gordon. (2006). *2006 State of the Future*. New York: American Council for the United Nations University.

Hart-Teeter. (2003). *The New E-Government Equation: Ease, Engagement, Privacy, and Protection*. Washington, DC: Council for Excellence in Government.

———. (2004). *From the Home Front to the Front Lines: America Speaks Out about Homeland Security*. Washington, DC: Council for Excellence in Government.

Haveman, D. D., and H. J. Shatz. (2006). "The Government Response: U.S. Port Security Programs and Financing Port Security." In *Protecting the Nation's Seaports: Balancing Security and Cost*, ed. J. D. Haveman and H. J. Shatz. San Francisco: Public Policy Institute of California. 233–256.

Hawken, P. (1993). *The Ecology of Commerce: A Declaration of Sustainability*. New York: HarperCollins.

Henton, D., J. Melville, and K. Walesh. (1997). *Grassroots Leaders for a New Economy*. San Francisco: Jossey-Bass.

Hermida, A. (2005). "Net Power Struggle Nears Climax." *BBC News Online*. news.bbc.co.uk/1/low/technology/4327928.stm.

Hubbard, R., and G. Paquet. (2005). "Betting on Mechanisms: The New Frontier for Federalism." *Optimum Online*, 35:1, 2–26.

———. (2006, September). "Re-inventer notre architecture institutionnelle." *Policy Options*. Montreal: IRPP.

IAAC (Information Assurance Advisory Council). (2002). *Protecting the Digital Society: A Manifesto for the UK*. London: Information Assurance Advisory Council.

Ignatieff, M. (2004). *The Lesser Evil: Political Dynamics in the Age of Terror.* Princeton: Princeton University Press.

Innovest. (2002). "Value at Risk: Climate Change and the Future of Governance." CERES Sustainable Governance Project Report.

Institute for Competitiveness and Prosperity. (2004). *Partnering for Investment in Canada's Prosperity.* Report presented at the Annual Meeting 2004 of the World Economic Forum, Davos, Switzerland. www.competeprosper.ca.

International Federation of Accountants. (2004). *Enterprise Governance: Getting the Balance Right.* New York: IFAC.

Ircha, M. C. (2003, spring). "Canadian Ports: A Critical Infrastructure Component." *Canadian Ports Magazine,* 14–21.

Information Technology Association of America (ITAA). (2005). "Transforming Procurement for the 21st Century in the County of Los Angeles, City of Los Angeles, and the Los Angeles Unified School District." Presentation by the Los Angeles Procurement Task Force.

Jacobs, J. 1992. *Systems of Survival.* New York: Random House.

JVSVN (Joint Venture Silicon Valley Network). (2005). *Regional Index 2005.* www.jointventure.org.

Keating, M., J. Loughlin, and K. Deschouwer. (2003). *Culture, Institutions, and Economic Development.* Cheltenham: Edward Elgar.

Kennedy, A. (2000). *The End of Shareholder Value: Corporations at the Crossroads.* Cambridge, MA: Perseus Publications.

Koch, C. (2003, March 15). "Your Open Source Plan." *CIO Magazine.* www.cio.com.

Langford, J., and J. Roy. (2006). "E-Government and Public-Private Partnerships in Canada: When Failure Is No Longer an Option." *International Journal of Electronic Business,* 4:2, 118–135.

Lau, E., ed. (2005). *E-Government for Better Government.* Paris: OECD.

Leganza, G. (2004). *Gains Sharing: Transformational Procurement.* Cambridge, MA: Forrester Research.

Lindsay, A., and G. Allen. (2005). "Developments in Public Affairs in Australia." *Journal of Public Affairs,* 5, 71–77.

Lodge, G., and B. Rogers. (2006). *Whitehall's Black Box: Accountability and Performance in the Senior Public Service.* London: IPPR.

Lowery, D. (2007). "Why Do Organized Interests Lobby? A Multi-Goal, Multi-Context Theory of Lobbying." *Polity,* 39:1, 29–54.

Maskell, P. (2000). "Social Capital and Competitiveness." In *Social Capital: Critical Perspectives,* ed. S. Baron, J. Field, and T. Schuller. Oxford: Oxford University Press. 223–254.

McGrath, C. (2005). *Lobbying in London, Washington, and Brussels: The Persuasive Communication of Political Issues.* New York: Edwin Mellin Press.

Miles, M., and J. Roy. (2001). "Corporate Governance as Culture in Industry and Government." *Optimum Online,* 31:1, 18–23.

Mintzberg, H. (1996, May–June). "Managing Government, Governing Management." *Harvard Business Review,* 75-83.

Mohammed, A., and S. Kehaulani. (2006, June 15). "Government Increasingly Turning to Data-Mining." *Washington Post,* www.washingtonpost.com.

Montana, J., A. Reamer, D. Henton, and K. Walesh. (2001). *Strategic Planning in the Technology-Driven World: A Guidebook for Innovation-Led Development.* Washington, DC: Collaborative Economics and the Economic Development Administration, US Department of Commerce.

Naim, M. (2006, May 28). "Borderline: It's Not about Maps." *Washington Post,* www.washingtonpost.com.

Naisbitt, J. (1994). *The Global Paradox.* New York: Morrow.

Nelson, M. R. (1998). "Government and Governance in the Networked World." In *Blueprint to the Digital Economy: Creating Wealth in the Era of E-Business,* ed. D. Tapscott, with A. Lowy and D. Ticoll. New York: McGraw-Hill. 274–298.

Neuhoff, K., and M. Grubb. (2006). "Allocation and Competitiveness in the EU Emissions Trading Scheme: Policy Overview." *Climate Policy,* 6:1, 5–28.

Niosi, J., and M. Banik. (2005). "The Evolution and Performance of Biotechnology Regional Systems of Innovation." *Cambridge Journal of Economics,* 29, 343–357.

OECD (Organization for Economic Cooperation and Development). (2001). "The Hidden Threat of E-Government: Avoiding Large Government IT Failures." Public Management Policy Brief 8. Paris: OECD.

———. (2002). *Territorial Review of Canada.* Paris: Territorial Reviews and Governance Division.

———. (2004). *The Security Economy.* Paris: OECD.

O'Harrow, R. (2004). *No Place to Hide.* New York: Free Press.

P. A. Knowledge. (2005). *In Sourcing Research.* London: ISiS Programme.

Paquet, G. (1996-97). "The Strategic State." *Ciencia Ergo Sum,* 3:3, 257–261 (part 1); 4:1, 28–34 (part 2); 4:2, 148–154 (part 3).

———. (1997). "States, Communities, and Markets: The Distributed Governance Scenario." In *The Nation-State in a Global Information Era: Policy Challenges,* ed. T. J. Courchene. The Bell Canada Papers in Economics and Public Policy 5. Kingston: John Deutsch Institute for the Study of Economic Policy. 25–46.

———. (1999). *Governance through Social Learning*. Ottawa: University of Ottawa Press.

———. (2002). *Ottawa 20/20 and Baroque Governance: A Report on the Smart Growth Summit of June 2001*. Ottawa: Centre on Governance.

———. (2005). *The New Geo-Governance: A Baroque Approach*. Ottawa: University of Ottawa Press.

Paquet, G., and J. Roy. (2004). "Smarter Cities in Canada." *Optimum Online*, 33:1, 2–20.

Paquet, G., J. Roy, and C. Wilson. (2004). "The River Runs through It: The Case for Collaborative Governance in the National Capital Region." In *Silicon Valley North: A High-Tech Cluster of Innovation and Entrepreneurship*, ed. L. Shavinina. Amsterdam: Elsevier. 223–239.

Patterson, P., and S. Biagi. (2003). *The Loom of Change: Weaving a New Economy in Cape Breton*. Cape Breton: University College of Cape Breton Press.

Pollitt, M. G. (2000). *The Declining Role of the State in Infrastructure Investment in the UK*. www.econ.cam.ac.uk/dae/repec/cam/pdf/WP0001.PDF.

Porter, M., with C. H. M Ketels, K. Miller, and R. T. Bryden. (2004). *Competitiveness in Rural US Regions: Learning and Research Agenda*. Cambridge, MA: Institute for Strategy and Competitiveness, Harvard Business School.

Public Policy Forum. (2002). *Bridging Two Solitudes: A Discussion Paper on Federal Industry – Government Relations*. Ottawa: PPF.

Putnam, R. (1994). *Making Democracy Work*. Princeton: Princeton University Press.

PWGSC. (2005). *Parliamentary Secretary Task Force: Government Wide Review of Procurement*. Ottawa: Government of Canada.

Reed, B. (2004). "Accountability in a Shared Services World." In *Future Challenges for E-Government*, ed. J. Halligan and T. Moore. Canberra: Government of Australia. 139–152.

Reid, J. (2004). "Holding Governments Accountable by Strengthening Access to Information Laws and Information Management Practices." In *E-Government Reconsidered: Renewal of Governance for the Knowledge Age*, ed. L. Oliver and L. Sanders. Regina: Canadian Plains Research Center. 87–104.

Rheingold, H. (2002). *SmartMobs: The Next Social Revolution*. New York: Perseus Publishing.

Roy, J. (1998). "Canada's Technology Triangle." In *Local and Regional Systems of Innovation*, ed. J. de la Mothe and G. Paquet. London: Kluwer Academic Publishers. 239–256.

———. (2003). "The Relational Dynamics of E-Governance: A Case Study of the City of Ottawa." *Public Performance and Management Review*, 26, 1–13.

———. (2006a). "E-Service Delivery and New Governance Capacities: 'Service Canada' as a Case Study." *International Journal of Services Technology and Management*, 7:3, 253–271.

———. (2006b). *E-Government in Canada: Transformation for the Digital Age*. Ottawa: University of Ottawa Press.

———. (2006c, July-August). "National Identity and Continental Interoperability: Does Canada Need a New I.D. Card?" *Policy Options*. Montreal: IRPP.

———. (2006d). "Security and Borders in a Digital Age: Implications for Canadian Government and North American Governance." *Journal of Borderland Studies*, 21:1, 87–107.

———. (2007). "E-Health in Ontario: A Multi-Dimensional Governance Transformation." *International Journal of Health Care Technology and Management*, 8:1-2, 66–84.

Savoie, D. J. (1999). *Governing from the Centre: The Concentration of Power in Canadian Politics*. Toronto: University of Toronto Press.

———. (2003). *Breaking the Bargain: Public Servants, Ministers, and Parliament*. Toronto: University of Toronto Press.

Sawatsky, J. (1987). *The Insiders: Power, Money, and Secrets in Ottawa*. Toronto: McClelland and Stewart.

Saxenian, A. (1994). *Regional Advantage*. Cambridge, MA: Harvard University Press.

———. (2002). "Transnational Communities and the Evolution of Global Production Networks: Taiwan, China, and India." *Industry and Innovation*, 93:3, 183–202.

Scalet, S. D. (2006, June 1). "Cyber-Security: A Job for Uncle Sam." *CIO Magazine*, 1–5.

Schacter, M., and T. Plumptre. (1999). *Public Good, Private Gain: A Study of Canadian Exemplary Companies and Their Relations with Government*. Ottawa: Institute on Governance.

Schumpeter, J. A. (1947). "The Creative Response in Economic History." *Journal of Economic History*, 7:2, 149–159.

Scott, M. (2004). "Building Institutional Capacity in Rural Northern Ireland: The Role of Partnership Governance in the LEADER II Programme." *Journal of Rural Studies*, 20, 49–59.

Silverstein, K. (2007, November). "Barack Obama Inc." *Harper's Magazine*. www.harpers.org/archive/2007/11/0081275.

Slack, E., L. Bourne, and M. S. Gertler. (2003). "Small, Rural, and Remote Communities: The Anatomy of Risk." Paper prepared for the Province of Ontario's Panel on the Role of Government.

Smith, K. (2006). "The Hollowing Out of Corporate Canada: Myth or Reality?" In *Perspectives*. Montreal: SECOR Consulting.

Solove, D. (2004). *The Digital Person: Technology and Privacy in the Information Age*. New York : NYU Press.

Sperling, E. (2006). "Valley Lobbying Pays Dividends." *Electronic News*. www.reed-electronics.com/electronicnews/article/CA6303941. html.

Stanbury, W. T. (1993). *Business-Government Relations in Canada: Influencing Public Policy*. Scarborough: Nelson Canada.

Steeves, V., and I. Kerr. (2005). "Virtual Playgrounds and Buddybots: A Data-Minefield for Tweens." *Canadian Journal of Law and Technology*, 4:2, 91–99.

Storper, M. (1997). *The Regional World: Territorial Development in a Global Economy*. New York: Guilford Press.

Stratos. (2003). *Building Confidence: Corporate Sustainability Reporting in Canada*. www.stratos-sts.com.

Strickland, L. S., and L. Hunt. (2005). "Technology, Privacy, and Homeland Security: New Tools, New Threats, New Public Perception." *Journal of American Society for Information Science and Technology*, Special Issue on Intelligence and Security Informatics, 56:3, 220–235.

Swedish Agency for Public Management. (2004). *Public Administration in the E-Society, Short Version*. Stockholm: Government of Sweden.

Tapscott, D., and D. Ticoll. (2003). *The Naked Corporation: How the Age of Transparency Will Revolutionize Business*. Toronto: Viking Canada.

TD Economics. (2006, June 22). *Creating the Winning Conditions for Public-Private Partnerships (P3s) in Canada*. www.td.com/economics.

Thurow, L. (1992). *Head to Head: The Coming Economic Battle among Japan, Europe, and America* Cambridge, MA: MIT Press.

Vining, A. R., M. D. Shapiro, and B. Borges. (2005). "Building the Firm's Political (Lobbying) Strategy." *Journal of Public Affairs*, 5, 31–45.

Wang, F., H. Zhang, and M. Ouyang. (2005). "Software Piracy and Ethical Decision Making Behaviour of Chinese Consumers." *Journal of Comparative International Management*, 8:2, 43–56.

Wayne, L. (2006, March 17). "Same Washington, Different Office: John Ashcroft Sets Up Shop as Well-Connected Lobbyist." *New York Times*, C1.

Weber, S. (2005). "The Political Economy of Open Source and Why It Matters." In *Digital Formations: IT and New Architectures in the Global Realm*, ed. R. Latham and E. Sassen. Princeton: Princeton University Press. 178–212.

Westlund, H. (2005). *The Social Capital of Regional Dynamics: A Policy Perspective*. Ostersund: National Institute for Working Life.

Witherall, W. (2000, September). "Corporate Governance: A Basic Foundation for the Global Economy." *OECD Observer*. www.oecdobserver.org/news/fullstory.php/aid/317.

Wonglimpiyarat, J. (2005). "What Are the Mechanisms Driving the Success of the US Silicon Valley?" *International Journal of Technology, Policy, and Management*, 5:2, 200–213.

Yankelovich, D. (1999). *The Magic of Dialogue: Transforming Conflict into Cooperation*. New York: Simon and Schuster.

Zinnbauer, D. (2004). "E-Government as Driver for More Institutional Transparency? A Closer Look at Interests, Policy Frames, and Advocacy Efforts." Research Memo 2, Social Science Research Council. www.ssrc.org

INDEX

CPSIA information can be obtained at www.ICGtesting.com
Printed in the USA
BVOW03s1800080913

330351BV00013B/51/P